The Lost Gospel of Judas

The Lost Gospel of Judas

SEPARATING FACT FROM FICTION

Stanley E. Porter & Gordon L. Heath

William B. Eerdmans Publishing Company

Grand Rapids, Michigan / Cambridge, U.K.

Wm. B. Eerdmans Publishing Co.
2140 Oak Industrial Drive N.E., Grand Rapids, Michigan 49505 /
P.O. Box 163, Cambridge CB3 9PU U.K.

Printed in the United States of America

12 11 10 09 08 07   7 6 5 4 3 2 1

Library of Congress Cataloging-in-Publication Data

Porter, Stanley E., 1956-
    The lost Gospel of Judas: separating fact from fiction /
    Stanley E. Porter & Gordon L. Heath.
        p.   cm.
Includes bibliographical references.
ISBN 978-0-8028-2456-1 (pbk.: alk. paper)
1. Gospel of Judas — Criticism, interpretation, etc.   I. Heath, Gordon L.
II. Title.

BS2860.J832P67   2007
229'.8 — dc22

                                                    2006036409

www.eerdmans.com

Contents

Contents

Preface

There has been plenty of hyperbolic language used of the *Gospel of Judas* recently. It is because of this hyperbole that we undertook to write this book. To put it quite honestly, as a New Testament scholar and a church historian we were surprised, if not bewildered, by the response to the *Gospel of Judas.* On the one hand, this was another in a long line of recent discoveries that was being hailed as the greatest discovery since, well, the last great discovery. On the other hand, it seemed that there were a lot of people who did not know what to think about this manuscript. There is no doubt that all the media attention contributed to the bewilderment.

As a result, we wrote this book to attempt to set the record straight. The *Gospel of Judas* is no doubt a relatively significant find from the fourth century, with possible implications for having been written and even translated as early as the second century. The *Gospel of Judas* does present a picture of Jesus that is foreign to the New Testament account which needs to be placed in its proper context. We have attempted to sift through all of this evidence and present the results of our examination in a readable format for those who are interested in such things.

We wish to thank a number of people for making this project possible. Each of the authors appreciates the work of the other. Team projects and collaboration do not always work as easily as has this one. We thank each other for being so agreeable to dividing the task, checking each other's work, and producing the volume in such an efficient manner. We wish also to thank our publisher, William B. Eerdmans of Grand Rapids, Michigan, for their willingness to publish this volume. We are thankful to Michael Thomson for the role that he has played in ensuring that this project was brought to completion and to John Simpson for his efficient editing. Lastly, but far from, well, leastly, we wish to thank our families for their support.

If this volume is able to shed light on the nature of the *Gospel of Judas*, the last in a long line of recent archaeological and textual studies, then it will have accomplished its purpose.

Initial Responses
to the Discovery of the
Gospel of Judas

The *Gospel of Judas*'s meteoric rise to become the topic of choice at water coolers, newsrooms, and talk shows was the result of a variety of inter-related factors. No doubt the professional marketing by the National Geographic Society contributed to the level of interest. Its TV documentary on the discovery of the document and its importance for our understanding of the events surrounding Christ's betrayal and crucifixion was certainly dramatic and sensational. The release of the document, TV show, and a number of books in the days leading up to Easter was also a significant factor in the interest shown toward the document. Most media during Easter spend some time exploring the events of Easter, and the release of the news about the discovery and the publication of the actual document were a natural time for media to pick up the story and run with it. The many articles and books published in the days surrounding the release of the discovery and document also meant that readers were presented with a wide variety of sources to read on the *Gospel of Judas*.

What should one think about the *Gospel of Judas?* What does the *Gospel of Judas* have to do with the traditional understanding of the Christian faith? While some respondents on the recent discovery have been reasonably subdued in their comments, others claim that the *Gospel of Judas* will revolutionize the Christian faith and provide a new understanding of Judas, Jesus and the events surrounding the crucifixion. The following is a brief summary of these claims.

1. The Media

The National Geographic Society's special documentary on the *Gospel of Judas* spared no efforts to draw in viewers. The trailer was filled with statements that alluded to the dramatic implications of the document. It asked the provocative question "will a dramatic discovery rewrite biblical history?" It went on to state that the newly discovered gospel would "tell a different story" from the one in the Bible, and was a story that could "challenge our deepest beliefs," turn the "story of Christ's betrayal on its head," and show that the villain was actually a "hero."[1] Near the end of the promo a voice stated that the contents of the document could be "explosive" and could create a "crisis of faith." While such language certainly was chosen for its marketing potential, the claims being made were startling and serious for anyone who held to a traditional understanding of the Easter narrative.

As was to be expected, the news media reported on the manuscript from the very first announcement of the discovery of the gospel in Paris, July 1, 2004.[2] As Easter 2006 approached and the date for the release of the National Geographic documentary and the actual text of the manuscript drew near, major daily papers reported on the newest find. Many of the headlines of newspapers were (perhaps understandably) quite sensational, with provocative questions such as "Was Judas a True Christian Hero?"[3] or "Did Jesus Ask Judas to Betray Him?"[4]

Dramatic eye-catching headlines aside, a significant amount of the reporting was helpful and presented a balanced view of the *Gospel of Judas*. The general pattern of reporting was no surprise; the basic facts of the find were outlined, and experts were sought on the significance of the discovery. In the most helpful articles, scholars in favor of the *Gospel of Judas* overturning the traditional understanding of the Christian faith

1. http://www.nationalgeographic.com/channel/gospelofjudas/index.html

2. For a summary of the early reports, see James M. Robinson, *The Secrets of Judas: The Story of the Misunderstood Disciple and His Lost Gospel* (San Francisco: HarperCollins, 2006), ch. 4.

3. *Globe and Mail* (April 7, 2006), A1.

4. *National Post* (April 7, 2006), A1.

were quoted, as were contrary positions from scholars who were not convinced that the new gospel had anything significant to contribute to the historical narrative. A good example of this relatively fair reporting can be found in the *New York Times* coverage on April 7, 2006.[5] The articles in this issue presented a balanced and informative picture of the *Gospel of Judas*. Other articles in different publications focused on specific aspects of the find. For instance, the *Dallas News* had an informative article that included commentary on the nature of second-century Gnosticism,[6] and the *Washington Post* had a piece on the discovery of the document.[7] The *Post* also had an online discussion with Marvin Meyer, a member of the nine-person Codex Advisory Panel assembled by the National Geographic Society and an expert on Gnosticism and the Nag Hammadi library.[8] While Meyer's views were not supportive of the traditional understanding of Judas, at least the *Post* sought to elevate the discussion by bringing in an expert.

An article in the *Chicago Tribune* is one example of a more critical approach to the church's traditional view of the past. Referring to the record of events surrounding Easter, the author states that "what evolved is an approved version of events, not necessarily the real version of events."[9] However, articles were also published in favor of the traditional understanding of events. The *Washington Times*, for instance, published an article that defended the traditional account against the attacks of the doubters and skeptics. Part of the article asked: "What is responsible for this flood of skepticism, heresy and outright denial of the biblical record? Why is there not a similar cul-

---

5. See John Noble Wilford and Laurie Goodstein, "In Ancient Document, Judas, Minus the Betrayal," *New York Times* (April 7, 2006), A1, 18; Laurie Goodstein, "Document Is Genuine, but Is Its Story True?" *New York Times* (April 7, 2006), A18.

6. Lauren F. Winner, "Judas as Mystical Good Guy," *Dallas News* (April 7, 2006). Retrieved from dallasnews.com.

7. Bradley S. Klapper, "Discovery of New Gospel No Fictional Tale," *Washington Post* (April 13, 2006). Retrieved from washingtonpost.com.

8. "Newly Translated Gospel Offers More Positive Portrayal of Judas," *Washington Post* (April 7, 2006). Retrieved from washingtonpost.com.

9. Charles M. Madigan, "Judas, Holy Week and the Faithful," *Chicago Tribune* (April 11, 2006). Retrieved from chicagotribune.com.

tural onslaught against other faiths? Only the suicidal would treat Islam in this way."[10]

What is noteworthy is that, in the midst of the evaluations of the actual discovery and its meaning, the National Geographic Society was taken to task for the nature of its involvement in the project and the way it promoted its findings. A *Los Angeles Times* editorial criticized the society for two things.[11] First, the National Geographic Society's promotion of the discovery had more "commercial zing than scholarly thoughtfulness." Second, the Society's willingness "to cut deals over a find whose legality is unclear, without being forthright about its role" in the purchase of the document was questionable. The *New York Times* echoed the same sentiments a few days later when it asked whether "calculated sensationalism and scholarly complicity in [the purchase of the document] were justifiable means to achieve these ends."[12]

Philip Jenkins argues that for nearly half a century "new findings in Jesus scholarship have been made widely available through the mass media, which clearly recognize the existence of a profitable general market." He goes on to claim that the media have most often "demonstrated a powerful if undiscriminating hunger for the latest critical claims and theories about the real Jesus and the hidden gospels." He made these claims over half a decade ago, in response to the media's coverage of other twentieth-century finds. In many respects the response of the media to this most recent discovery simply confirms his assertion. It should be noted, though, that Jenkins does not claim that the media are necessarily trying to attack traditional Christianity (although in certain cases it may be):

> If the media err, they do so through misunderstanding rather than malice, and a genuine failure to understand the nature of the scholarly

10. Cal Thomas, "The Gospel of Unbelievers," *The Washington Times* (April 12, 2006). Retrieved from washingtontimes.com.

11. Editorial, "Judas Deal, 2,000 Years Later," *LA Times* (April 13, 2006). Retrieved from latimes.com.

12. Peter Steinfels, "A Debate Flares on Betrayal," *New York Times* (April 15, 2006). Retrieved from nytimes.com.

profession: the media have an understandable preference for ideas that appear daring and newsworthy.[13]

The consequence of such sensational and often "hostile" coverage, however, is that the media become more than just commentators on the discovered documents and instead become shapers of a "new mythology" of Christian origins — one that is radically different from any traditional understanding.

2. Books

The reintroduction of the *Gospel of Judas* to the world was aided by the publication of three books, two published by the National Geographic Society and one by HarperCollins. All three attempt to explain the discovery of the document, its content and authenticity, and its significance. These books are immensely important, if for no other reason than they have had the first chance to shape the discussion of the document.

A. *The Gospel of Judas*

Rodolphe Kasser, Marvin Meyer, and Gregor Wurst are the editors of *The Gospel of Judas*, which provides an English translation of the text of the actual *Gospel of Judas*, along with commentary and analysis by the editors and Bart Ehrman.[14] Kasser is professor emeritus in the Faculty of Arts at the University of Geneva, Switzerland, and has a significant amount of experience in the study of Greek and Coptic texts. Meyer is professor of Bible and Christian Studies at Chapman University, Orange, California, and has spent a great deal of time on the texts of the Nag Hammadi library. Wurst is the professor of the History of Christianity in the Faculty of Catholic Theology at the University of Augsburg, Germany, and an

13. Philip Jenkins, *Hidden Gospels: How the Search for Jesus Lost Its Way* (Oxford/New York: Oxford University Press, 2001), 178-79.

14. Rodolphe Kasser, Marvin Meyer, and Gregor Wurst, eds., *The Gospel of Judas from Codex Tchacos* (Washington: National Geographic, 2006).

5

experienced Coptic scholar. Kasser, Meyer, and Wurst were all involved in the translation of the *Gospel of Judas*.[15] Ehrman is the author of *Lost Christianities*, a book that will be referred to in subsequent chapters. While none of these four scholars seem to fit into the conservative camp, all four are certainly qualified to comment on the discovery. This volume makes the most important scholarly contribution to discussion of the *Gospel of Judas*, and we respond to a number of its claims throughout this book.

Kasser's chapter on the story of the discovery and eventually publication of the document is helpful for those interested in a brief but informative account of the clandestine efforts to sell the document and bring it to the attention of scholars and the public.[16] More germane to our purposes, however, are the chapters on the significance of the document.

Meyer's chapter seeks to explain the Gnostic components of the *Gospel of Judas* and place them in the standard categories of Gnostic research.[17] The conclusions of this chapter are really only of interest to those well-versed in Gnostic studies, and his somewhat esoteric thesis is that the *Gospel of Judas* belongs to an early school of Sethian Gnostic thought. His basic argument is that certain phrases, ideas, and parallel constructions are similar enough to other Sethian Gnostic writings to place the document within the school. We provide our own discussion of Gnosticism in Chapter Two below.

Wurst's chapter deals with the early Christian attitudes to the *Gospel of Judas*.[18] The key question that he grapples with is whether or not the *Gospel of Judas* referred to by Irenaeus is the same work. He notes that the strongest argument against it being the same is that the recent discovery

15. Rodolphe Kasser, Marvin Meyer, and Gregor Wurst, in collaboration with François Gaudard, "The Gospel of Judas," in Kasser, Meyer, and Wurst, eds., *Gospel of Judas*, 17-45.

16. Rodolphe Kasser, "The Story of Codex Tchacos and the Gospel of Judas," in Kasser, Meyer, and Wurst, eds., *Gospel of Judas*, 47-76.

17. Marvin Meyer, "Judas and the Gnostic Connection," in Kasser, Meyer, and Wurst, eds., *Gospel of Judas*, 137-69.

18. Gregor Wurst, "Irenaeus of Lyon and the Gospel of Judas," in Kasser, Meyer, and Wurst, eds., *Gospel of Judas*, 121-36.

does not have references to Cain or other antiheroes mentioned by Irenaeus. But he argues that Irenaeus most likely never saw the *Gospel of Judas* and only knew of it through hearsay. Wurst concludes that, in fact, they are one and the same. Regarding what can be concluded from Irenaeus, Wurst writes:

> What can be deduced from the account of Irenaeus with certainty is that the Cainites read a *Gospel of Judas* and that they referred to it in support of their understanding of the act of betrayal as a mystery. This implies that Judas was portrayed in that gospel as the disciple of Jesus "acquainted with the truth as no others were" and that the act of the betrayal must have been interpreted, in terms of a Gnostic view of history of salvation, as part of the "dissolution of all earthly and heavenly things."[19]

What clinches it for Wurst is that the *Gospel of Judas* contains both these elements: Judas is presented as one with special knowledge of Jesus' true identity, and some of the prophetic language links Judas with the plan of salvation. The fact that there is no other reference to any other *Gospel of Judas* in antiquity is further support for his position.

On the basis of the conclusion that the recent find is the *Gospel of Judas* that Irenaeus referred to, Wurst dates the writing of the gospel before A.D. 180 (the date when Irenaeus referred to it). Given a reference in the *Gospel of Judas* to the New Testament book of Acts, Wurst also concludes that the *Gospel of Judas* was written after A.D. 90-100, the date when many scholars conclude Acts was written. We consider this question below, in Chapter Three.

The most problematic chapter for those with a more conservative approach to the historical narrative of the New Testament Gospels is Ehrman's.[20] Ehrman's influence on the shaping of how the *Gospel of Judas* is understood cannot be underestimated. Besides writing this chapter,

---

19. Wurst, "Irenaeus of Lyon," 128.

20. Bart D. Ehrman, "Christianity Turned on Its Head: The Alternative Vision of the Gospel of Judas," in Kasser, Meyer, and Wurst, eds., *Gospel of Judas*, 77-120.

very early in the process he was invited by the National Geographic Society to bring his expertise in early Christian history to the team of scholars who were translating the document. He wrote the Foreword to *The Lost Gospel*, the other book published by the Society to tell the story of the new find (discussed below). His comments have also been sought by numerous media sources, and quotations by Ehrman permeate a significant number of newspaper articles.

Neither Ehrman's summary of the Gnostic elements of the *Gospel of Judas* nor his brief outline of other twentieth-century finds of Gnostic material is problematic; his comments on these topics in this chapter are quite helpful. What is problematic are his assumptions and conclusions regarding the battle between orthodoxy and heretical movements in the early church — assumptions that have a direct bearing on how one determines the significance of the *Gospel of Judas* today. No one doubts that there were theological conflicts in the early church. But Ehrman does not see one side as necessarily right (the orthodox) and others wrong (the heretics):

> We have long known about these debates, and the *Gospel of Judas* allows us to see one side of them even more clearly — one of the sides that ended up losing. Every side laid claim to sacred books supporting its point of view; all insisted that these views came straight from Jesus, and through him from God. But only one side won. This was the side that decided which books should be considered Scripture, and that wrote the Christian creeds that have come down to us today.[21]

"Orthodoxy" (he always puts this term in quotation marks to reinforce that there was no real difference in terms of claims to truth from the heretics) was simply the fortuitous winner of the theological battles. When the New Testament was being formed, he argues, and more and more other gospels were being circulated, the question of what was to be included and excluded was dealt with by one group (the "orthodox") simply "overwhelming all the others" in numbers and power. The result was

---

21. Ehrman, "Alternative Vision," 103.

that all other texts that differed from those of the power-block were eliminated. For Ehrman, the *Gospel of Judas* was one of those alternative views of Jesus that had been eliminated by the heresy hunters. Its discovery, therefore, is a great find that can be seen as a no less orthodox version of events than the other allegedly orthodox texts. We directly respond to Ehrman's hypothesis in Chapter Nine.

B. *The Lost Gospel: The Quest for the Gospel of Judas Iscariot*

This, the second book published by the National Geographic Society on the discovery of the *Gospel of Judas*, seeks to outline the history of the discovery of the lost gospel.[22] The author, Herbert Krosney, is an award-winning writer and maker of documentary films who has considerable experience in historical projects. The Foreword was written by Ehrman, and his influence can be seen in certain comments throughout Krosney's text.

Krosney's account of how the *Gospel of Judas* was discovered and eventually brought into the public eye is an interesting and informative glimpse into the shady world of illegal trading in antiquities. However, the labyrinth that the document went through and survived is not our concern here. What is of interest are some of the assumptions and statements made by Krosney regarding the significance of the find, and most of these can be found in his chapter eleven.

Krosney claims that the early Christians did not have a "definitive" faith or Bible for well over three hundred years.[23] He even claims that the New Testament was not complete until the Council of Trent in 1545. Like Ehrman, Krosney stresses the diversity of the early church ("competing Christian sects"), points out that there were thirty or more other gospels to choose from, and notes that the four traditional Gospels "disagree on specific historical facts or the sequence of events in the biblical narrative."[24] He also claims that Irenaeus, finding himself surrounded by her-

22. Herbert Krosney, *The Lost Gospel: The Quest for the Gospel of Judas Iscariot* (Washington: National Geographic, 2006).

23. Krosney, *The Lost Gospel*, 182.

24. Krosney, *The Lost Gospel*, 183.

esy, was the one who "came to the fore" and helped to define what was acceptable or orthodox. Irenaeus, he argues, then went on to pursue those who differed from his personal idea of what was heresy. The problem, for Krosney, was that the target of the heresy-hunting Irenaeus was the Gnostics, a group who were widespread "throughout much of Christendom"[25] and who believed "wholly in the general truth of their concepts."[26] The conversion of Constantine in the early fourth century, and Athanasius's formalizing of the canon, meant that the orthodox had won the battle, and their views became the norm. The losers' writings simply disappeared over time — and one such writing to disappear was the *Gospel of Judas*.

C. *The Secrets of Judas: The Story of the Misunderstood Disciple and His Lost Gospel*

The Preface of James Robinson's book includes some harsh words for those on the "inside" of the National Geographic work on the *Gospel of Judas*. He claims that "those on the inside have been bought off (no doubt with considerably more than thirty pieces of silver) and sworn to silence." He goes on to claim that his "outsider's" version of the events surrounding the recent discovery is not "expurgated, sanitized, [or] cleaned up to make it an appetizing story,"[27] unlike, he suggests, the account presented by the National Geographic Society. How much of this is personal "sour grapes" is not clear, but Robinson certainly has no love for the way in which others have held a monopoly on ancient texts, and his fear seems to be that the original text of the *Gospel of Judas* will be kept secret by an elite group of scholars rather than released to the entire academic community for study. The secrecy surrounding the release of the *Gospel of Judas* only seems to confirm his fears.

Robinson is qualified to comment on the discovery for several reasons. First, he is the founding director emeritus of the Institute for Antiq-

---

25. Krosney, *The Lost Gospel*, 193.
26. Krosney, *The Lost Gospel*, 195.
27. Robinson, *Secrets of Judas*, vii.

uity and Christianity and professor emeritus at Claremont Graduate University, Claremont, California. He has authored numerous works on early Christianity and was the general editor of *The Nag Hammadi Library in English*. Second, he had knowledge of the *Gospel of Judas* back in 1983, when he was contacted about possibly purchasing it (he claims that he did not know at that time what the document actually was). The deal fell through, and Robinson's involvement — but not interest — was terminated.

Robinson's book is primarily an attempt to provide details on Judas (as portrayed in the New Testament and church history), the shady dealings surrounding the sale of the document, and the significance of the new-found gospel. The weakness of the book is that he does not know some of the inside dealings, and, at the time of writing, did not have access to the actual text (which means that he could only speculate about what it contained). The strength of the book is that his "outsider" status makes him free to criticize the process of its release to the public. For instance, he makes it clear that the original text should not be monopolized by the owners — something that an "insider" may find it difficult to say (at least in public and in print).

Despite his "outsider" status, however, Robinson shares many assumptions with the above-mentioned authors. He distances himself from what he calls the "standard conservative prejudice in favor of limiting oneself to the canonical Gospels to the exclusion of the noncanonical Gospels."[28] He also uses polemical terms such as "heresy-hunting church fathers" that present a negative image of the traditional orthodox leaders and church.[29] What is encouraging about Robinson's approach, however, is that he holds off making extravagant claims about the significance of the gospel until he has seen it himself. He even provides a brief summary and critique of some of the preposterous claims made in the media and states that the *Gospel of Judas* is a second-century apocryphal gospel that probably tells us about second-century Cainite Gnostics, not about what happened in A.D. 30.[30]

---

28. Robinson, *Secrets of Judas*, 73.
29. Robinson, *Secrets of Judas*, 53.
30. Robinson, *Secrets of Judas*, 177.

3. Conclusion

What should one think about the *Gospel of Judas?* What does the *Gospel of Judas* have to do with the traditional understanding of the Christian faith? On the positive side, there were many cases of thoughtful and balanced reporting on the discovery. However, the problem that many traditional or conservative Christians have with the media response to the *Gospel of Judas* is that the often sensationalized message is corrosive to their deeply held convictions about the Easter events, and the only published books on the matter assume many things that seem ultimately to undermine their cherished convictions. The sympathy for the Gnostics (versus the heresy-hunting orthodox), the assumption that orthodoxy is not connected in any way to "truth," but instead is simply the side that won the theological battles, and the reliance on critical methods that do not necessarily take a text at face value contribute to an interpretation of the new find that is contrary to a traditional understanding of Christianity. Accordingly, so the argument goes, the *Gospel of Judas* will revolutionize the Christian faith and provide a new understanding of Judas, Jesus, and the events surrounding the crucifixion.

To make matters worse, once extravagant claims are made, it is hard to counter such claims. Referring to the media's response to previous findings, Jenkins notes:

> Once a group of scholars decided to make their extravagant claims in the public arena, rather than merely in academe, they found that they possessed every conceivable advantage. Advocates of the hidden gospels were dealing with topics in which the media already had a powerful interest, and they presented their conclusions in terms which could not fail to win the sympathy of both journalists and readers, as they ably mobilized so many contemporary prejudices. Failure was all but impossible: even the most forceful conservative counterattack could be turned to advantage, by suggesting that the very depth of hostility proved the strength and dangerousness of the radical arguments. At every stage, the methods, and working assumptions of the

media resulted in preferential, uncritical treatment for the heretics, past and present.[31]

What this means for any scholars who seek to go against the grain of popularized media portrayals of the *Gospel of Judas* is that they must work uphill. In an age when diversity is praised, exclusive claims to truth seem to be from the Dark Ages (and the cause of world conflicts), and postmodern perspectivalism dominates epistemological assumptions, they must also take on the unenviable task of defending the actions of people portrayed as believing in the truthfulness of orthodox Christianity and the falseness of Gnostic versions. Not an easy task.

31. Jenkins, *Hidden Gospels*, 203-4.

CHAPTER ONE

Judas in Scripture and Church History:
A Brief Introduction

One of the best places to begin a response to the recent proposals regarding the *Gospel of Judas* is with Judas himself. Is Judas the widely misunderstood person that recent media proposals seem to endorse, or is the traditional understanding of Judas a more accurate assessment? In this chapter, we examine what the New Testament itself and church history have to say about Judas.

1. Judas in the New Testament

A number of New Testament passages speak of Judas. The earliest written is from Paul. There are also passages in the Gospels, beginning with Mark's Gospel, probably the earliest of the canonical Gospels, followed by statements in Matthew and Luke. Material on Judas in John's Gospel provides information not found in the Synoptic Gospels. The book of Acts contains additional information on Judas's death. We will take a brief look at all of these.

There have been a number of recent attempts to reinterpret these New Testament passages on Judas in order to reassess his guilt regarding the death of Jesus. One of the key distinctions to make when evaluating the validity of these attempts is the important difference between knowing, permitting, and causing an action and how these levels of knowledge have a relationship to individual responsibility. The issue also re-volves around the meaning of the Greek verb often translated "betray" and whether it is better translated simply "hand over" or whether there is a more insidious intent implied in this handing over.[1] The following is a concise evaluation of Judas in the New Testament and church history and a brief critique of attempts to reassess the traditional interpretation of Judas's guilt.

A. 1 Corinthians 11:23

This is probably the earliest New Testament account of Jesus' betrayal. There are two elements of this text to note for our discussion regarding Judas. The first is that there are two uses of the verb "hand over" in this verse. The verse says that "I received from the Lord, what also I handed over to you, that the Lord Jesus in the night in which he was handed over took bread. . . ." The first use of the verb indicates that Paul is passing on to the Corinthians information. The second use speaks of the specific night in which Jesus was handed over. Paul may be indicating that it was God who was ultimately responsible for Jesus being handed over (cf. Romans 8:32, where Paul says that God handed Jesus over for us), but the mention here of a specific night and the occasion of the last supper with his disciples points to the actual details surrounding his being handed over by Judas. The context does not specifically say that the handing over of Jesus was a betrayal, nor does the account mention Judas by name. As a result, William Klassen concludes that the developing Christian tradition at this point did not know of Jesus being betrayed by Ju-das.[2] While it is true that Paul does not mention Judas by name, one can-not make too much of this.[3] He does not mention by name any of the disciples except Peter, James, and John. Paul does say that the handing

1. This is the contention of William Klassen (*Judas: Betrayer or Friend of Jesus?* [Minne-apolis: Fortress, 1996], 48), followed by James M. Robinson, *The Secrets of Judas: The Story of the Misunderstood Disciple and His Lost Gospel* (San Francisco: HarperCollins, 2006), 42-43.

2. Klassen, *Judas,* 51.

3. One certainly cannot conclude that the Gospels, though written later, do not con-tain historically accurate information. The Gospels were a form of ancient biography.

over of Jesus was caused by human sin, however. In Romans 4:25, Paul says that Jesus was handed over because of "our transgressions." The sin of the specific betrayer who acted on that night of the last supper is included within the sins of all humanity — he certainly is not exempt from that sinfulness. Thus, though Paul does not mention Judas by name as the one who handed over Jesus, he knows of a sin-motivated betrayal that took place on the last night Jesus spent with his disciples.

B. The Synoptic Gospels

i. Mark 14:10-11, 18, 21, 41-49 There are a number of passages in Mark's Gospel, probably the earliest of the Gospel accounts,[4] that refer to Judas. Some scholars wish to decipher different layers in the tradition regarding Jesus.[5] The danger with such an approach is that they may find that what they identify as the earliest tradition conforms to the pattern they are ultimately seeking. The approach taken here is to consider the entire narrative of the Gospel and see what the text says about Judas.

The first scene in which Judas figures in a significant way follows after the incident of the woman anointing Jesus' feet (Mark 14:3-9). Mark says that some of the disciples were indignant over her waste of the expensive perfume. John identifies the disciple who reacted in this way as Judas, who was a thief and intending to hand over Jesus (John 12:4-6). This makes sense of Judas's subsequent going to the chief priests in order to arrange Jesus' arrest (Mark 14:10-11). The chief priests promised Judas money for this act, and after that he sought an opportune time to hand over Jesus. Klassen takes Judas's action not as that of a betrayer but as that of an informer, who is trying to get Jesus to meet with the proper temple authorities.[6] But Klassen (nor we) cannot be sure of what Judas's real motivation(s) was. The outcome, however, speaks for itself. The role

---

4. Most scholars believe that Mark's Gospel was written first and that Matthew and Luke used Mark's Gospel. Luke (1:1-4) says that he consulted earlier sources. Matthew and Luke also had access to other independent sources.

5. This is the approach that Klassen takes through his book, *Judas*.

6. Klassen, *Judas*, 66-73.

of noble informer is difficult to support when Judas accepts money for the role, performs it clandestinely, and does things that end up working against Jesus and his followers, as we shall see below.

When the disciples gather with Jesus for their last supper together, Jesus indicates his knowledge that one of them will hand him over (Mark 14:18). At first, this statement might seem ambiguous, as if Jesus approved of the action, or even that he and Judas had contrived this together. However, Jesus' subsequent statement corrects this misimpression. In one of his "son of man" statements[7] regarding his death, Jesus states that his being handed over is part of the prophesied plan of God, but also "woe to that man through whom the son of man is handed over. It would be good for him if that man was not born" (Mark 14:21). This pronouncement of woe over Judas's actions is a clear condemnation of them as antagonistic to the "son of man," that is, Jesus, even if anticipated and prophesied. In other words, the handing over appears to be a betrayal.

After the last supper, Jesus goes to the garden of Gethsemane and prays with his disciples. After he has prayed for the third time he sees Judas coming, and he alludes to the words that he uttered earlier, when he states that "the son of man is being handed over into the hands of sinners" (Mark 14:41). If Judas were simply orchestrating a desired meeting between Jesus and the temple authorities, what follows next would have been totally unnecessary. Judas is accompanied by armed men, and he tells them which one to seize and take away securely, which they do.[8] Even if we are not meant to see it as a dangerous situation, one of the disciples certainly did, and he drew his sword to defend Jesus (John identifies this one as Peter; John 18:10), and then they all fled.

ii. Matthew 26:14-16, 21-25, 47-56 Matthew's account is similar to Mark's, but adds certain details. For example, Matthew has a more explicit account of the dialogue between Judas and the chief priests, which makes it clear that Judas is bargaining to hand over Jesus for money

---

7. "Son of man" is the way that Jesus often refers to himself in the Gospels. By using it, Jesus is equating himself with the "one like a son of man" referred to in Daniel 7:13.

8. Klassen conveniently leaves Mark 14:44 out of his account because he claims it was not a part of the tradition before Mark. See Klassen, *Judas,* 80.

(Matthew 26:15). This certainly calls Judas's motives into questions. These motives are further compromised by noting that Judas was looking for the right time to hand over Jesus (Matthew 26:16) — but the right time for whom? Certainly not Jesus, as the ensuing arrest makes clear, which takes place at night with swords and clubs. Jesus, too, notes that he has been in the temple regularly teaching and this has provided an opportunity for a meeting, if a meeting is all that were desired (Matthew 26:55). Earlier, at the last supper, when Jesus converses with Judas, Judas asks whether he is the subject of the woe, and Jesus answers "you have said" (Matthew 26:25). This statement is ambiguous, but it probably focuses responsibility for Judas's actions on Judas. Jesus tells him that he himself is the one who has undertaken the betrayal.[9]

iii. Luke 22:3-6, 21-23, 47-53   Whatever one may think about Judas's motives from Mark and Matthew's Gospels, Luke is clear that Judas was up to no good. He states that "Satan entered into Judas" (Luke 22:3), and this led to his going to the chief priests to discuss how he might hand Jesus over to them. When Judas comes to have Jesus arrested, not only does Jesus observe that he was with them in the temple (as he does in Matthew), but he links the actions taking place with the powers of darkness (Luke 22:53). This is consonant with Luke's description of Satan entering into Judas.

C. John's Gospel

In John's Gospel there are a number of references to Judas worth considering: 6:64-71; 12:1-8; 13:1-30; 17:12; and 18:1-11. When Jesus first introduces the idea of his being handed over, he equates the one who would do this with those who do not believe (John 6:64). Jesus states the two sides of the dilemma: he has chosen his followers, the twelve, and he knows that one of them is a devil. Just in case we as readers do not understand who this is, John clarifies by stating that Jesus meant Judas Iscariot (John 6:71).

9. Klassen, *Judas*, 101-2.

During the last supper, John tells us, the devil was already at work in the heart of Judas (John 13:2) so that he would hand over Jesus. As Jesus washes his disciples' feet, he recognizes that not all of them are clean (13:10), knowing that one of his closest followers is intent on handing him over (13:11). Later, Jesus states outright that he knows that one of his followers will hand him over. The ground has already been laid for this handing over to be seen as an act of betrayal because, according to John, it is motivated by the devil acting upon and within Judas. This is certainly how the disciples take it when they begin to inquire who it is. Thus, when Jesus dips the morsel and gives it to Judas, he is acknowledging what the author interprets explicitly for us: "Satan then entered into him" (13:27). Jesus then bids Judas to do quickly what he is about to do. Some have interpreted this to mean that Jesus is in some way complicit in Judas's actions or even that Judas is simply doing what Jesus has asked or compelled him to do. That interpretation clearly does not fit the context — the attribution of motivation for this action is ascribed by John to the devil or Satan.

When Jesus is later praying his farewell prayer on behalf of the disciples, he recognizes that he has kept them safe — except for one, whom he calls the son of perdition. He acknowledges that what is about to happen is in fulfillment of Scripture, but clearly he distances himself from the motivation for the actions and labels Judas as cursed for his actions (John 17:12).

D. The Death of Judas

There are two accounts of the demise of Judas in the New Testament. Each makes clear that, no matter what Judas may have thought or pretended his motives were for handing over Jesus, something went horribly wrong. Even if one believes that a well-intentioned handing over for the purposes of mutual understanding between Jesus and the chief priests was the original motivation (giving the benefit of the doubt to at best a questionable idea), it clearly ended up a betrayal that led to the death of Jesus. Judas's remorse indicates his recognition of this as well.

i. Matthew 27:1-10 Matthew records that Judas saw that Jesus had been condemned by the Jewish leaders. He felt remorse and tried to return the thirty pieces of silver to them. The link of the silver with the act of handing Jesus over is further reinforced in this scene. Judas then acknowledged that he had sinned by handing over an innocent person. The handing over to death of an innocent person strikes us as being the very definition of betrayal. After this, Matthew says that Judas went and hanged himself, and the chief priests took his returned money and bought a field for paupers' burials. The field was called the "field of blood."

ii. Acts 1:16-20 In Acts, when the time comes to replace Judas, Peter offers a brief account of Judas's ill fortunes. There are several important components to Peter's explanation. First, he states that Judas benefited from the acquiring of a field with the reward of wickedness. Second, he states that Judas became swollen and then burst open, and all his guts poured out. Third, he states that the field was called "field of blood."

There is a tendency by some scholars to play these two accounts of Judas's death off against each other.[10] They actually have much more in common than some recognize.[11] The Acts account does not say that Judas bought the field, but that he benefited from its acquisition — it provided a place for him to kill himself. The two accounts are also compatible with hanging, and certainly with suicide.[12] Matthew says this explicitly, but the account in Acts probably records the effect of hanging in the hot Palestinian sun until one bloated and burst (a condition that can happen to decomposing bodies). Both Matthew and Acts agree that the field (the words for "field" are different, but they are partial synonyms) was called "field of blood," whether that was its proper name or not (it certainly was descriptive).[13] Lastly, both agree that Judas's unrighteousness or sinfulness motivated this outcome.

---

10. Kim Paffenroth, *Judas: Images of the Lost Disciple* (Louisville: Westminster/John Knox, 2001), 21-22; Robinson, *Secrets of Judas,* 47.

11. Klassen, *Judas,* 169-70.

12. See Robinson, *Secrets of Judas,* 47.

13. Paffenroth, *Judas,* 11-14.

E. Summary

A number of clear findings can be summarized from this brief perusal of passages about Judas in the New Testament. One is that the rendering of "betray" for what Judas did to Jesus is a right and proper one — if not from the standpoint of his initial motivation (we do not accede to this, but simply posit it for the sake of argument), at least by the time the action is complete. This is what motivates Judas to take his life in a horrific guilt-ridden end to a sinful act. There is also a consistency to the New Testament evidence regarding Judas. Even if Jesus did know what Judas was going to do, and what Judas did had in some sense to be done as prophecy stated, Judas is clearly held accountable for his actions as an act of betrayal. He is labeled by the Gospel writers as being filled by the devil or Satan, his actions are labeled as being sinful or wicked, his motivation is impurely motivated by money, he is overcome with remorse and guilt, and he is held accountable for his actions. Those who would seek to revise our view of Judas may be right that his act of denial was one of many acts of denial during Jesus' arrest (the text is clear that all but a few of the disciples fled, and Peter denied Jesus outright). However, faithfulness to the earliest traditions of the texts of the New Testament does not support a reinterpretation that absolves Judas of sin or culpability in Jesus' arrest and death. The Gospel accounts from Mark to John confirm this account in detail. And what about Judas's responsibility when Jesus prophesied Judas's betrayal? Peter denied Jesus three times, even though Jesus knew in advance and prophesied that he would do so. Peter's actions still required repentance on his part and forgiveness that Jesus was willing to give. For Judas, it seems, there was no repentance and no forgiveness, because there was only remorse over sinfully motivated betrayal.

2. Judas in Church History

Out of the twelve disciples, Judas is the disciple who "has attracted the most sustained attention on the part of the church as well as historians of folklore and culture."[14] The following is a very brief summary of the various ways in which Judas has been portrayed in the church and in society after the first century.

A. The Traitor

The most common portrayal of Judas was as a traitor, and, as one source states, he has "been regarded with universal abhorrence in the Christian church."[15] This should come as no surprise, since the New Testament consistently portrays him as the one who betrayed Jesus. One second-century portrayal of Judas attributed to Papias (ca. A.D. 130) provides a graphic and not very compassionate picture of the (by then) infamous traitor:

> Judas wandered in this world, a great example of impiety. His flesh swelled so much that where a cart went through easily, he was not able to go through, not even the mass of his head; they say that his eyelids swelled so much that he could not see any light at all, and his eyes could not be seen even with a doctor's instruments, because they had sunken so far from the surface of his face. His genitals were more enlarged and unsightly than any other deformity, while blood and worms flowed from all over his body, necessarily doing great harm just by themselves. After many such tortures and punishments, they say that he died on his own property, and that on account of the stench the place is desolate and uninhabited even until now, and that even today no one can go through that place without stopping up his nose with his hands, because the stench of his flesh spread out over the land so much.[16]

Cyril of Syria's fourth-century homily on the Easter event also provides a clear picture of just how evil Judas was in the minds of many:

14. Klassen, *Judas*, 4.

15. "Judas Iscariot," in F. L. Cross, ed., *The Oxford Dictionary of the Christian Church* (London: Oxford University Press, 1958), 750.

16. As quoted in Paffenroth, *Judas*, 23.

At eventide Judas left the dining hall and the disciples, who had been depressed, remained behind in deepest peace. The vessel of wrath left his master and the devious one separated himself from his associates. The dining chamber rejoiced that the darkness had lifted from the Twelve and the goat had fled; now the wheat had been purged of weeds and the vines of the vineyard of wild grapes. The owl, which praised darkness, left the doves alone and flew out squawking. The house became bright with light in which the hidden sun remained with its beams; it rejoiced because the cursed viper, who had destroyed himself, had departed. As that one left his head was heavy, his face was glowing red, his countenance distorted, his heart was racing, his whole being disturbed, his teeth chattering, his knees shaking. His mind had left him, his powers of deliberation gone from him.[17]

These themes of heinous crime and the evil of Judas were repeated in many ways throughout the Middle Ages. In fact, Paffenroth notes that the Middle Ages was perhaps the "heyday for the depiction of Judas as the epitome of evil and the most powerful object lesson in the dire results of sin."[18] One extreme example is that of a preacher that preached on Judas every Sunday for ten years![19] One literary example is the scene in Dante's *Divine Comedy* that describes the very bottom of hell and Satan chewing on three sinners. The one suffering most is Judas:

That soul up there who suffers most of all,
my guide explained, is Judas Iscariot:
the one with head inside and legs out kicking.[20]

His betrayal of Christ had placed him at the bottom of hell, into the jaws of Satan, and had gained him the dubious distinction of the greatest of sinners.

17. As quoted in Klassen, *Judas*, 178.
18. Paffenroth, *Judas*, 26-27.
19. Klassen, *Judas*, 18-19.
20. As quoted in Paffenroth, *Judas*, 27-28.

B. Sympathy for Judas

For those alarmed with the claim of the *Gospel of Judas* that Judas may not have been such a bad guy, it may come as a surprise to know that not everyone has seen Judas as the villain. Despite the negative portrayals of Judas throughout the church's history, there have also been a variety of portrayals of Judas that have been sympathetic toward him. For instance, Klassen records the contents of one Dominican preacher's sympathetic sermon about Judas:

> Judas who betrayed and sold the Master after the crucifixion was overwhelmed by a genuine and saving sense of remorse and tried with all his might to draw close to Christ in order to apologise for his betrayal and sale. But since Jesus was accompanied by such a large crowd of people on the way to the mount of Calvary, it was impossible for Judas to come to him and he said to himself: Since I cannot get to the feet of the master, I will approach him in my spirit at least and humbly ask him for forgiveness. He actually did that and as he took the rope and hanged himself his soul rushed to Christ on Calvary's mount, asked for forgiveness and received it fully from Christ, went up to heaven with him and so his soul enjoys salvation along with all elect.[21]

Klassen goes on to note that the Dominican's views were considered heretical. However, this sympathetic portrayal of Judas was not the only one. Paffenroth devotes an entire chapter to ways in which Judas was an object of admiration and sympathy throughout the church's history.[22]

In the twentieth century, sympathy in certain quarters for Judas has continued. One of the more recent popular portrayals of Judas was in the movie *Jesus Christ Superstar*. Besides the work of Robinson, *The Secrets of Judas*, noted above, an even more recent example of a sympathetic portrayal of Judas is William Klassen's *Judas: Betrayer or Friend of Jesus?* In this

21. Klassen, *Judas*, 7.
22. Paffenroth, *Judas*, ch. 4.

work Klassen seeks to show how the New Testament does not justify the "betrayer" judgment of Judas. Instead, he argues that Judas was acting in obedience to Jesus and that the (mis)treatment of Judas may be rooted in Christian difficulties with Judaism.[23]

3. Conclusion

The Judas of the *Gospel of Judas* does not have anything in common with the scriptural and traditional depictions of Judas. The New Testament, despite protests by recent critics to the contrary, depicts Judas as the betrayer of Jesus, as the one who orchestrated his being handed over to his death at the hands of the Jewish and Roman authorities. This is also the traditional view of Judas throughout church history. However, the *Gospel of Judas* has a great deal in common with other sympathetic interpretations of Judas's life. In the *Gospel of Judas,* Judas is not portrayed as a traitor but rather as one doing the bidding of Jesus. The traditional view has been discarded, and in its place is a radical revision of the biblical story.

---

23. "Is it too much to suggest that it was not disobedience but rather obedience which brought that about and that there are indeed two parallel lines between Jesus and Judas? The inability of the church to give him a fair hearing may have had historical roots in her relationship with her sister faith, Judaism." See Klassen, *Judas,* 192 and our response to Klassen, pp. 15-21 above.

CHAPTER TWO

Gnosticism: What Was It,
How Widespread Was It, and
Why Was It a Problem for the Church?

Discussion of the *Gospel of Judas* inevitably involves discussion of the ancient belief system called Gnosticism. As we saw in our introduction above, those who discuss the *Gospel of Judas* recognize that this document reflects the ancient teaching of a group called Gnostics. In this chapter, we provide a summary and assessment of Gnosticism in relation to the early church.

1. What Was It?

Gnosticism (the "g" is silent) has become quite popular today due to a variety of factors, such as the discovery of Gnostic texts at Nag Hammadi in Egypt in 1945[1] and popular novels such as Dan Brown's *The Da Vinci Code* that refer quite positively to ancient Gnosticism. The discovery of the Gnostic *Gospel of Judas* has added even more popular interest in Gnosticism. But what exactly was Gnosticism?

The term itself is "largely the creation of modern historical scholarship," and early Christians usually referred to each Gnostic group by the name of its particular leader.[2] One difficulty in trying to come to grips

---

1. We discuss the Nag Hammadi documents in more detail in Chapter Four.
2. Jaroslav Pelikan, *The Emergence of the Catholic Tradition (100-600)* (Chicago: Univer-

with Gnosticism is that it was an incredibly diverse movement. One early church father referred to it as a many-headed hydra of Greek mythology.[3] A more contemporary scholar says the following about the diversity of Gnosticism:

> Defining Gnosticism is an extraordinarily difficult task, since modern writers use the term to cover a variety of speculative religious phenomena. These phenomena are encountered from Gaul in the West to Iran in the East, from the first century of our era to at least the ninth.... There are systems which ambivalently love and scorn the world and systems which explicitly hate the world. The systems include notions related to Zoroastrianism, Babylonian religion, Judaism, Hellenistic philosophy and religion, and Christianity. How are we to define Gnosticism as a whole? The Christian Clement of Alexandria has provided us with a systematic analysis of the various names given the Gnostic sects. Some derived their names from their founder: Valentinians, Marcionites, Basilidians. Others were named after their place of origin (Peratikoi) or their nationality (Phrygians). In other cases, the names came from their activities (Encratites, "the continent ones"), their doctrines (Docetists, Haimatitoi [otherwise unknown]), the objects of their enthusiasm or worship (Cainites, Ophites [from *ophis*, serpent]), or from their immoral practices (certain Simonians called Entychites, from their promiscuity). It is not clear whether they applied these names to themselves or not. Probably, most of the names were given them by their opponents. In any event, the varieties of names illustrate the variety present among the sects.[4]

---

sity of Chicago Press, 1971), 81. A treatment arranged according to its major figures is found in Hans Jonas, *The Gnostic Religion: The Message of the Alien God and the Beginnings of Christianity* (second ed.; Boston: Beacon, 1963).

3. Irenaeus, *Against Heresies* 1.30 in *Ante-Nicene Fathers* 1 (Christian Literature, 1885; reprint, Peabody: Hendrickson, 2004), 310 (page citations are to the reprint edition). Unless noted otherwise, all references in footnotes to early Christian writings below are from the *Ante-Nicene Fathers* edition.

4. Robert M. Grant, *Gnosticism and Early Christianity* (second ed.; New York: Columbia University Press, 1966), 6-7.

Despite such incredible diversity, some elements common to all make it possible for us to speak of Gnosticism as a movement or category of thought. Some of the key convictions and characteristics of Gnosticism were as follows.[5]

A. Special "Gnosis"

Gnōsis is a Greek word that is usually translated "knowledge" or "understanding." Gnostics were those who believed that they had gained access to special knowledge that would help them achieve salvation and escape the material world. This special (and often secret) knowledge was revealed by God and transmitted to others by an elite group of followers. In regards to Christian Gnosticism, it was believed that Jesus brought a special message from God (*gnōsis*) and revealed it to a select group of followers. Christian Gnostics also claimed that orthodox Christians did not have this knowledge; only they, the Christian Gnostics, did. In other words, they were the true apostles, with the true knowledge of Christ's teaching. One author argues that this knowledge is the first and most important point in defining Gnosticism. He claims that "it is a religion of saving knowledge, and the knowledge is essentially self-knowledge, recognition of the divine element which constitutes the true self."[6] Along with this key belief went a wide variety of myths and practices.

B. Matter/Spirit Dualism

Gnosticism was based on the philosophical foundation of Platonism, which made a sharp distinction between the ideal and the material or the eternal and the now. For Gnostics, the physical or material was something evil that needed to be escaped from; only the spiritual was good. Salvation, therefore, was not about a physical resurrection (as or-

---

5. See Kurt Rudolph, *Gnosis: The Nature and History of Gnosticism* (trans. Robin McL. Wilson; San Francisco: Harper, 1987).

6. Grant, *Gnosticism and Early Christianity*, 10.

thodox Christians claimed), but about a freeing or liberating of one's spirit from one's body. Consistent with the principle that matter was evil, Gnostics believed that while Christ was an emissary of God, he in no way had a real human body, nor did he die. His human appearance was just that — an appearance but not a material reality.

C. Creation by a Lesser God

Gnostics made a distinction between the creator god (the "Demiurge") and the true, supreme, unknowable Divine Being. As Riemer Roukema notes, Gnostics elevated the highest God "so high above the material world that he is not regarded as its creator."[7] Only lesser gods could be involved in lesser things such as the creation of matter — lesser gods such as the Demiurge. The Demiurge was one of a series of emanations, or aeons, that descended or emanated from the Divine Being. This lesser god created the material world.

Various humans, however, still had a divine spark within them, and this divine spark needed to be freed from material existence. The way to freedom, or redemption, for these elites was through special knowledge and the practices that went with it. Consequently, a part of the Gnostic worldview was a sense that there was a cosmic struggle going on, and that ultimately matter will be dispensed with and the elite will have their spirits freed to exist in a truly spiritual universe. One of the best accounts of this cosmic struggle is found in the Gnostic writing entitled *The Apocryphon of John*. Classic Gnostic literature, according to one scholar, teaches:

> **Act I: The emanation of the spiritual universe**
> At the beginning of the myth is the perfect, ultimate, and omnipotent divine source, or "first principle," of all further existence; it is ineffable and beyond description. . . .

---

7. Riemer Roukema, *Gnosis and Faith in Early Christianity: An Introduction to Gnosticism* (Harrisburg: Trinity, 1999), 105.

Act II: The creation of the material universe

After the emission of the spiritual universe has been completed, in order for creation to continue beyond the limit of spiritual existence the activity of a "craftsman" or "maker" of the world is introduced; his name is Ialdabaoth. . . .

Act III: The creation of Adam, Eve, and their children

The rest of the myth concerns the efforts of wisdom, aided by higher aeons of the spiritual universe, to regain the stolen power. Although Ialdabaoth is lured into surrendering it, in the process Adam and then a human race are created; and the stolen power becomes dispersed in the successive generations, whom Ialdabaoth's offspring enslave by creating destiny and malevolent spirits of deception. . . .

Act IV: The subsequent history of the human race

In gnostic eyes the final act of the drama is still in progress. A heavenly savior has been sent to "awaken" gnostic humanity, to give them acquaintance (gnosis) with themselves and god, to free their souls from destiny and from bondage to the material body, and to teach them how to escape the influence of the malevolent rulers.[8]

For people looking for answers and purpose in the midst of often inexplicable evil, the Gnostic myth of the cosmic struggle (of which there were many variations) promised redemption from evil and gave a degree of hope and purpose.

Most Gnostics saw the God portrayed in the Old Testament as not the true God, but a lesser god — perhaps the Demiurge. For how could the Divine Being be involved with matter? And how could the true God do the things that are described in the Old Testament (such as wipe out the Canaanites)?

---

8. Bentley Layton, *The Gnostic Scriptures* (Garden City: Doubleday, 1987), 14-17.

D. Allegorical Interpretations of the Bible

What was also common among Gnostics was their allegorical interpretation of the Bible. While an allegorical interpretation was practiced by both orthodox Christians and the Gnostics, the Gnostic interpretations of Scripture were overwhelmingly allegorical. Of course, finding the "true" meaning, or "secret" meaning, and a fascination with numbers, parallels, etymologies and hidden meanings in the Scriptures were consistent with the Gnostic emphasis on special knowledge.

2. How Widespread Was It?

It is difficult to know how widespread the movement was, but in the second century the church had to deal with serious Gnostic threats. One such threat was that of the Gnostic sect of the Valentinians. According to Irenaeus (a fervent opponent of the movement), Valentinus was a native of Egypt who came to Rome ca. A.D. 140. He was one of the most important and influential Gnostics that the church had to deal with, and the movement he established could still be found in the eastern and western churches up until the seventh century.

Another important figure influenced by Gnostic ideas was Marcion (died ca. A.D. 160). He arrived in Rome ca. 140 and, after starting to form a group of followers, was excommunicated in 144. In the years that followed he established a wide network of churches and followers, and his movement was a serious threat to the church in the later part of the second century. One of his convictions was that the creator God, or Demiurge, of the Old Testament was not the God of the New Testament. His desire to purge the Christian scriptures of any reference to the Jewish God was one of the key factors that forced the church to define its canon.

There are two ways to get a sense of how big a problem Gnosticism was for the church. First, one can simply outline the number of Gnostic texts in circulation in the second and third centuries. Second, one can look at the energy spent writing in response to Gnosticism. In both cases, the impression is that for those in the catholic or orthodox church Gnosticism was a "clear and present danger."

31

A. The Number of Gnostic Writings

A simple listing of the contents of the Nag Hammadi library shows the difficulty of the task that faced opponents of Gnosticism. How many of these works were in circulation in the early centuries of the church's life cannot be known; but the number of texts that survived provides a glimpse of the extent of the problem.

The Prayer of the Apostle Paul
The Apocryphon of James
The Gospel of Truth
The Treatise on Resurrection
The Tripartite Tractate
The Apocryphon of John
The Gospel of Thomas
The Gospel of Philip
The Hypostasis of the Archons
On the Origin of the World
The Exegesis of the Soul
The Book of Thomas the Contender
The Gospel of the Egyptians
Eugnostos the Blessed
The Sophia of Jesus Christ
The Dialogue of the Savior
The Apocalypse of Paul
The First Apocalypse of James
The Second Apocalypse of James
The Apocalypse of Adam
The Acts of Peter and the Twelve Disciples
The Thunder, Perfect Mind
Authoritative Teaching
The Concept of Our Great Power
The Discourse on the Eighth and Ninth
The Prayer of Thanksgiving
The Paraphrase of Shem

The Second Treatise of the Great Seth
Apocalypse of Peter
The Teachings of Silvanus
The Three Steles of Seth
Zostrianos
The Letter of Peter to Philip
Melchizedek
The Thought of Norea
The Testimony of Truth
Marsanes
The Interpretation of Knowledge
A Valentinian Exposition
On the Anointing
On Baptism A
On Baptism B
On the Eucharist A
On the Eucharist B
Allogenes
Hypsiphrone
Fragments
Trimorphic Protennoia
On the Origin of the World
The Gospel of Mary
The Sophia of Jesus
The Act of Peter[9]

As can be seen in this list, matters were made even more difficult for the orthodox church by the fact that many of the Gnostic texts claimed apostolic authorship,[10] and the genres of what would become the New Tes-

9. List from James M. Robinson, ed., *The Nag Hammadi Library in English* (San Francisco: Harper and Row, 1988), xiii-xiv. This is just one library. There are other Gnostic texts as well. Layton (*Gnostic Scriptures*, xxvi) has a list of published Gnostic manuscripts which numbers about sixty-four works.

10. It should be noted that using someone else's name on a written work was not uncommon in that period, even though it was not considered morally acceptable. Such

tament writings were copied. To the unaware reader, Gnostic texts could easily be seen as orthodox texts (or vice versa). This potential for confusion was a serious problem for those concerned with preserving the apostolic message unchanged from how it had been originally received.

B. Literature in Response to Gnosticism

The response of church leaders was vigorous and substantial. A sample listing of some of the written works that dealt with Gnosticism reveals the energy expended to refute what was seen in all its varieties to be a deadly heresy. The following works dealt in whole or in part with Gnosticism.[11]

Justin Martyr (ca. 100-165)	*Apology, Dialogue with Trypho*
Irenaeus (ca. 130-200)	*Against Heresies*
Clement of Alexandria (ca. 150-215)	*Stromateis*
Tertullian (ca. 160-220)	*Against Marcion,*
	Against the Valentinians,
	On the Flesh of Christ,
	On the Resurrection of the Flesh
Hippolytus (ca. 170-236)	*Refutation of All Heresies*
Eusebius (ca. 260-340)	*Ecclesiastical History*
Epiphanius (ca. 315-403)	*Panarion*

Gerard Vallee argues that the three most important anti-Gnostic writers were Irenaeus, Hippolytus, and Epiphanius. The main anti-Gnostic writings of all three authors have survived (Justin had a work that dealt with all the many heresies, but it was lost), and all battled with every heresy they knew (unlike other authors who only took on a specific

---

writings are called "pseudepigrapha," and the purpose behind using someone else's name was to connect the work to a recognized authority and thus to increase the importance and authority of the work.

11. For a helpful anthology of anti-Gnostic writings, see Arland J. Hultgren and Steven A. Haggmark, eds., *The Earliest Christian Heretics: Readings from Their Opponents* (Minneapolis: Fortress, 1996).

heresy). In fact, it appears that these three authors' works were standard sources for the development of anti-heresy writings even into the Middle Ages.[12]

3. Why Was It a Problem for the Church?

Why invest so much time refuting Gnostics inside and outside the church? What was it about Gnostic teaching that these church leaders found to be so wrong? One way to answer these questions is to look at the comments of one of the critics of Gnosticism.[13]

In the work *Against Heresies* (ca. 182-88), Irenaeus sought to address the many Gnostics who had infiltrated the church. His aim (apparently unsuccessful) was twofold: "(1) to render it impossible for any one to confound Gnosticism with Christianity, and (2) to make it impossible for such a monstrous system to survive, or ever to rise again."[14] Irenaeus began by warning his readers that they should be careful, for the Gnostics made their teaching "appear to the inexperienced . . . more true than the truth itself," partly because the Gnostics used language that appeared to be Christian though, as Irenaeus stated, their sentiments were not.[15] He provided a myriad number of examples of how the Gnostics ignored the natural sense of Scripture and twisted it to fit their preconceived notions. The following long quotation provides a sense of the methodology that Irenaeus found simply unacceptable:

> They [Gnostics] tell us, however, that this knowledge has not been openly divulged, because all are not capable of receiving it, but has been mystically revealed by the Saviour through means of parables to

12. Gerard Vallee, *A Study in Anti-Gnostic Polemics: Irenaeus, Hippolytus, and Epiphanius* (Waterloo: Wilfrid Laurier University Press, 1981), 1-6.

13. Whether Irenaeus was correct in all his assumptions and conclusions regarding Gnosticism is another question. The desire here is simply to show how he saw the issues.

14. "Introductory Note to *Irenaeus Against Heresies*," in *Ante-Nicene Fathers* 1, 310. Page references are to this edition.

15. Irenaeus, *Against Heresies* 1, Preface.

those qualified for understanding it. This has been done as follows. The thirty Aeons are indicated . . . by the thirty years during which they say the Saviour performed no public act, and by the parable of the labourers in the vineyard. Paul also, they affirm, very clearly and frequently names these Aeons, and even goes so far as to preserve their order, when he says, "To all the generations of the Aeons of the Aeon." Nay, we ourselves, when at the giving of thanks we pronounce the words, "To Aeons of Aeons" (for ever and ever), do set forth these Aeons. And, in fine, wherever the words Aeon or Aeons occur, they at once refer them to these beings. The production, again, of the Duodecad of the Aeons, is indicated by the fact that the Lord was *twelve* years of age when He disputed with the teachers of the law, and by the election of the apostles, for of these there were twelve. The other eighteen Aeons are made manifest in this way: that the Lord [according to them] conversed with His disciples for eighteen months after His resurrection from the dead. They also affirm that these eighteen Aeons are strikingly indicated by the first two letters of His name [*Iēsous*], namely *Iota* and *Eta*. And, in like manner, they assert that the ten Aeons are pointed out by the letter *Iota*, which begins His name; while for the same reason, they tell us the Saviour said, "One *Iota*, or one tittle, shall by no means pass away until all be fulfilled." They further maintain that the passion which took place in the case of the twelfth Aeon is pointed at by the apostasy of Judas, who was the twelfth apostle, and also by the fact that Christ suffered in the twelfth month.[16]

In tedious detail Irenaeus goes on to illustrate the many other Gnostic approaches to reading the Scriptures. What they all have in common is a fascination with numbers, parallels, etymologies, and hidden meanings. In Irenaeus's opinion, such an approach to the Scriptures was to "disregard the order and the connection of the Scriptures, and so far as in them lie, dismember and destroy the truth."[17] What the Gnostics did

16. Irenaeus, *Against Heresies* 1.3.
17. Irenaeus, *Against Heresies* 1.8.

was very much like one who dismantles a work of art and recreates something entirely different from the original:

> when a beautiful image of a king has been constructed by some skill-ful artist out of precious jewels, [the Gnostics] ... then take this like-ness of the man all to pieces, ... re-arrange the gems, and so fit them into the form of a dog or a fox, and even that poorly executed; and ... then maintain and declare that *this* was the beautiful image of the king which the skillful artist constructed.[18]

In other words, the Gnostics eventually destroyed the meaning of the orig-inal authors. In Irenaeus's opinion, a fascination with numbers, parallels, etymologies and hidden meanings in the Scriptures was not a way to get at the real meaning of the Scriptures and of the essence of the Christian faith.

It is clear what specific doctrines Gnostic teaching undermined. In fact, even today scholars of Gnosticism agree that the vision of the Gnos-tic version of the Christian faith was radically different from the ortho-dox Christian faith. The following summary by W. H. C. Frend makes it clear what doctrines would suffer if Gnostics had their way:

> The danger with which the teaching of Valentinus and Basilides con-fronted orthodox Christianity needs no emphasis. The Old Testament was rejected.... The denial of the human element in the Savior and his suffering, death and resurrection struck at the heart of Christianity. There was no place for a doctrine of the Trinity, for there was no place for the Holy Spirit. As one critic of the early Gnostic systems pointed out, "strange opinions concerning the grace of Jesus Christ" led to the rejection of Christian morality ... [also] how could those who did not believe in the reality of Christ's body offer a valid Eucharist? More-over, the dualistic approach to the universe, inevitable if the universe was controlled by beings not "of God," induced fatalism in the individ-ual's moral outlook.[19]

18. Irenaeus, *Against Heresies* 1.8.
19. W. H. C. Frend, *The Early Church* (Minneapolis: Fortress, 1991), 54.

Basically every doctrine that was associated with Christianity would have been threatened by Gnostic teaching. Suffice it to say here that the lines were clearly drawn, and, in the minds of the early defenders of the faith, the church had to resist, or die.

4. Conclusion

Gnosticism, though broad and diverse in its range of beliefs, developed its own set of core beliefs that proved to be a direct threat to orthodox Christianity. The Gnostics were selective in what they believed or included within their belief systems. They did so by an allegorical method of interpretation of Scripture that allowed them to be selective in the beliefs that they incorporated. As a result, a number of early church writers, especially Irenaeus, responded to Gnosticism and argued against it. People like Irenaeus believed that Gnosticism struck at the very fundamentals of the Christian faith and therefore needed to be both intellectually refuted and rigorously opposed.

CHAPTER THREE

The Early Church and the
Gospel of Judas

The discovery of the *Gospel of Judas* is a significant find, but as the previous chapter indicates, it is simply one among many other Gnostic writings. There may even be more discoveries in the years to come. However, since our interest is specifically in the newly discovered document, this chapter will outline how the *Gospel of Judas* was received by the orthodox church up until it "disappeared."

1. Early Church References

A. Irenaeus (ca. 130-200)

Irenaeus was born ca. A.D. 130 in Smyrna, Asia Minor, and was made bishop of Lyons (France) in ca. 178. Tradition has it that, when he was a child, he heard Polycarp teaching. Since Polycarp was most likely a disciple of John, this places Irenaeus only one generation away from the first apostles — such a close connection to John would have given Irenaeus a unique position of authority when determining the message of the original apostles. Irenaeus played an important role in settling a dispute over the dating of Easter and was involved in establishing orthodoxy in the churches. He stressed many doctrines, including the canon of Scripture (especially the four Gospels Matthew, Mark, Luke, and John), monotheism, and the incarnation. He was also concerned about the spread of heresy and wrote extensively on the subject.

For many in the twenty-first century, innovation, change, and personal choice are all esteemed and sought after, and to be called an "original" or "innovative" thinker is a compliment. For Irenaeus, however, to be an innovator with the gospel was a bad thing. As one writer notes, he would have been "deeply offended had it been suggested to him that he was an original thinker."[1] In fact, for Irenaeus, the problem with the Gnostics and other heretics was that they had deviated from the tradition passed down from the first apostles. This conviction that one needed to stay true to the teaching of the apostles considerably shaped his response to heretics.

Irenaeus's most substantial work was *Against Heresies*, written ca. 182-88. It was originally written in Greek, but the earliest complete version of it that remains is a fourth-century Latin translation. One editor of his works states that *Against Heresies* "is one of the most precious remains of early Christian antiquity."[2] The work is divided into five smaller books that are all a part of the whole. Perhaps it is best to let Irenaeus describe his outline and the purpose of these five books. His introductory comments in book five provide a description of the entire project:

> In the four preceding books, my very dear friend, which I put forth to thee, all the heretics have been exposed, and their doctrines brought to light. . . . Then I have pointed out the truth, and shown the preaching of the Church, which the prophets proclaimed (as I have already demonstrated), but which Christ brought to perfection, and the apostles have handed down, from whom the Church, receiving these [truths], and throughout all the world alone preserving them in their integrity. . . . Then also — having disposed of all questions which heretics propose to us, and having explained the doctrine of the apostles, and having clearly set forth many of those things which were said and

1. Denis Minns, *Irenaeus* (Washington: Georgetown University Press, 1994), 132.
2. "Introductory Note to *Irenaeus Against Heresies*," in *Ante-Nicene Fathers* 1 (Christian Literature, 1885; reprint, Peabody: Hendrickson, 2004), 311.

done by the Lord in parables — I shall endeavor, in this the fifth book of the entire work . . . to exhibit proofs from the rest of the Lord's doctrine and apostolical epistles . . . [so as to] furnish thee with large assistance against the contradictions of the heretics, as also to reclaim the wanderers and convert them to the Church of God, to confirm at the same time the minds of the neophytes, that they may preserve steadfast the faith which they have received, guarded by the Church in its integrity, in order that they be in no way perverted by those who endeavor to teach them false doctrines, and lead them away from the truth.[3]

While Irenaeus may not have always accurately portrayed the heretical movements, his *Against Heresies* is a fascinating account of one man's attempt to steer the church away from heresy. Due to its blow-by-blow account of every last heresy that Irenaeus could identify, it is also very tedious and difficult to read at times. Not every heresy that he wrote on was Gnostic, but many would have fit that description. One of the groups that he identified was the Cainites, and it was in his dealing with the Cainites that Irenaeus made the earliest known reference to the *Gospel of Judas:*

Others again declare that Cain derived his being from the Power above, and acknowledge that Esau, Korah, the Sodomites, and all such persons, are related to themselves. On this account, they add, they have been assailed by the Creator, yet no one of them has suffered injury. Sophia was in the habit of carrying off that which belonged to her from them to herself. They declare that Judas the traitor was thoroughly acquainted with these things, and that he alone, knowing the truth as no others did, accomplished the mystery of the betrayal; by him all things, both earthly and heavenly, were thus thrown into confusion. They produce a fictitious history of this kind, which they style the Gospel of Judas.[4]

3. Irenaeus, *Against Heresies* 5 Preface.
4. Irenaeus, *Against Heresies* 1.31.

This reference is important for both what it says and what it does not say about the *Gospel of Judas*. It does not tell us who actually wrote the document, for Irenaeus only states that the Cainites "produce" a copy of it (and that could mean a variety of things). Irenaeus does not tell how many copies were in circulation, how popular it was within the Cainites and among groups outside their movement, or whether he had actually seen and read the document. And his words do not tell us whether the recently discovered *Gospel of Judas* is the same one he refers to. But they do tell us that a *Gospel of Judas* was written before ca. A.D. 180 (when Irenaeus wrote *Against Heresies*), was used by a group called the Cainites, and contained what Irenaeus considered heretical teaching.

Irenaeus's citation also tells us a bit about the group that used the document to support and propagate its views. The Cainites seemed to be a group of Gnostics who did not view the Old Testament God as the true God.[5] Instead, they supported and extolled the virtues of those who had opposed his work, such as Esau, Korah, and the Sodomites. Since Judas fits that description, he would have been esteemed among the Cainites, and the gospel in his name would have provided one more Gnostic text that helped to teach this view. According to Wurst, Irenaeus portrayed the Cainites as believing that Judas's deed was "a 'mystery' [that led] . . . to the dissolution of all earthly and heavenly things, that is, of all the works of the 'maker' or ruler of this world."[6] In other words, Judas's action was seen by the Cainites as a noble act to thwart the actions of the lesser or evil god and showed how he sought to serve the true and higher being.

B. Tertullian (ca. 160-220)

Tertullian was one of the most important Western, or Latin, theologians of the early church. Based in North Africa (one of the locations where the early church experienced considerable success), he sought to defend

---

5. The references to Cain in the New Testament (1 John 3:12; Jude 11–19) may indicate that this group had pre-Christian origins or at least very early origins.

6. Gregor Wurst, "Irenaeus of Lyon and the Gospel of Judas," in Rodolphe Kasser, Marvin Meyer, and Gregor Wurst, eds., *The Gospel of Judas from Codex Tchacos* (Washington: National Geographic, 2006), 124.

Christians against accusations that they were not good citizens, to protect the church against heretics by teaching true doctrine, and to call the church to pure and holy living. Later in his life, he joined the Montanists, an apocalyptic and ascetic Christian movement deemed heretical for its excesses.

Many of Tertullian's writings have survived, and in these works we can see that he dealt extensively with ethical issues, practical and doctrinal matters, and the threat of heresy. His *Five Books Against Marcion* and *Against the Valentinians* provide a detailed treatment of Gnosticism, but in these two works he makes no reference to the *Gospel of Judas*. However, there is a reference to the Cainites in his opening paragraph in *On Baptism*. It reads:

> Happy is our sacrament of water, in that, by washing away the sins of our early blindness, we are set free and admitted into eternal life! A treatise on this matter will not be superfluous; instructing not only such as are just becoming formed (in the faith), but them who, content with having simply believed, without full examination of the grounds of the traditions, carry (in mind), through ignorance, an untried though probable faith. The consequence is, that a viper of the Cainite heresy, lately conversant in this quarter, has carried away a great number with her most venomous doctrine, making it her aim to destroy baptism.[7]

Certainly Irenaeus made a connection between the Cainites and a *Gospel of Judas,* but we are left wondering if Tertullian did. The absence of any reference to a *Gospel of Judas* here may mean that he did not know about the gospel, or it may simply mean he did not see fit to refer to it. Tertullian also does not even tell us how or why the Cainites were such a threat. On the more positive side, this reference does inform us that the Cainites were perceived to be such a threat by Tertullian that he felt he had to address their attempts to "destroy baptism."

7. Tertullian, *On Baptism*, 1.1, in *Ante-Nicene Fathers* 3 (Christian Literature, 1885; reprint, Peabody: Hendrickson, 2004).

C. Pseudo-Tertullian

One work that has been linked to Tertullian is *Against All Heresies*. However, the consensus today is that *Against All Heresies* was not written by Tertullian.[8] In fact, Jerome (ca. 342-420) stated that it was written by a bishop named Victorinus Petavionensis who died as a martyr in ca. 303.[9] Regardless of who wrote it, the work contains a reference to the Cainites and Judas that needs to be noted:

> Moreover, also, there has broken out another heresy also, which is called that of the Cainites. And the reason is, that they magnify Cain as if he had been conceived of some potent Virtue which operated in him; for Abel had been procreated after being conceived of an inferior Virtue, and accordingly had been found inferior. They who assert this likewise defend the traitor Judas, telling us that he is admirable and great, because of the advantages he is vaunted to have conferred on mankind; for some of them think that thanksgiving is to be rendered to Judas on this account: viz., Judas, they say, observing that Christ wished to subvert the truth, betrayed Him, in order that there might be no possibility of truth's being subverted. And others dispute against them, and say: Because the powers of this world were unwilling that Christ should suffer, lest through His death salvation should be prepared for mankind, he, consulting for the salvation of mankind, betrayed Christ, in order that there might be no possibility at all of the salvation being impeded, which was being impeded through the Virtues which were opposing Christ's passion; and thus, through the passion of Christ, there might be no possibility of the salvation of mankind being retarded.[10]

This passage tells us a bit about the Cainites, but not about the *Gospel of Judas*, though now that we have the *Gospel of Judas* we can see similarities

---

8. One needs to be careful about how much authority one gives to the "consensus today" on any issue. Many majorities in the past have held to wrong and hurtful ideas. In other words, truth is not always on the side of the majority.

9. Jerome, *Lives of Illustrious Men* 53.

10. *Against All Heresies* 2, in *Ante-Nicene Fathers* 3.

between it and what Pseudo-Tertullian was describing. The author may have known of the gospel, but we simply cannot know either way. However, as Wurst notes, according to this passage there seemed to be among the Cainites two different interpretations of Judas's actions.[11] One stated that Judas kept Jesus from "subverting the truth" by betraying him. What this means is not totally clear. The other interpretation was that Judas's actions insured that Jesus died, thus keeping the lesser gods from impeding the plan of salvation. Again, what this means is not totally clear. What is clear, however, is that in either case Judas's actions were esteemed and he was a hero.

D. Hippolytus (ca. 170-236)

As noted above, Vallee considers Hippolytus one of the three most important anti-Gnostic writers in the early church. Not much is known about Hippolytus, but it is clear that he was one of the most important church theologians of the third century. In his *Refutation of All Heresies*, Hippolytus briefly refers to the Cainites but does not mention the *Gospel of Judas*.[12]

E. Epiphanius (ca. 315-403)

Epiphanius lived as a monk in Egypt until he returned to Judea in ca. 333, where he founded a monastery. In 367, he became bishop of Salamis on Cyprus, and he served in that capacity for close to forty years. He was active in the theological disputes of his day and was an ardent defender of Nicene orthodoxy at councils and in his various travels.

Epiphanius's most famous work is entitled the *Panarion* (meaning "medicine chest"). The *Panarion* was basically a handbook written in ca. 374-77 that listed and refuted eighty heretical teachings. It was in this work that he referred to the *Gospel of Judas*, and, like Irenaeus, he did so in the context of dealing with the Cainites. The following is a lengthy quotation, but it provides a sense of Epiphanius's view of the gospel:

11. Wurst, "Irenaeus of Lyon," 126.
12. Hippolytus, *Refutation of All Heresies* 8.13.

Those called Cainites get the name of their sect from Cain, for they admire Cain and take him as their father. . . . They say that Cain is from the stronger power and the dominion from above, as are also Esau, the company of Korah, and the Sodomites, while Abel is of the weaker power. [They consider?] them all praiseworthy and their kin. They boast of being related to Cain, the Sodomites, Esau, and Korah. These, they say, are of the perfect knowledge from above. For this reason, they say, although the maker of this world devoted himself to their annihilation, he could in no way harm them, for they were hidden from him and transported to the upper aeon whence the strong power is. Wisdom let them come in to herself, for they belonged to her. For this reason they say that Judas knew quite well what concerns these matters. They consider him their kinsman and count him among those possessing the highest knowledge, so that they also carry about a short writing in his name which they call the *Gospel of Judas*. . . . These fables they mix in with the mischievous ignorance they teach, advising their disciples that every man must choose for himself the stronger power and separate himself from the inferior and feebler, namely the one which made heaven, the flesh, and the world, and pass above to the highest regions through Christ's crucifixion. For it was for this reason, they say, that he came from above, that a strong power might be made active in him which would triumph over the weaker power and hand over the body. Now some of them teach this, but others say something else. Some of them say that it was because Christ was wicked that he was betrayed by Judas, because he, Christ, wanted to distort what pertains to the law. They admire Cain and Judas, as I said, and they say: For this reason he betrayed him, because he wanted to destroy sound teachings. But others of them say: Not at all; he betrayed him, although he was good, because of his [Judas's] knowledge of heavenly things. For, they say, the archons knew that if Christ were given over to the cross, their weak power would be drained. Judas, knowing this, bent every effort to betray him, thereby accomplishing a good work for our salvation. We ought to admire and praise him, because through him the salvation of the cross was prepared for us and the revelation of things above occasioned by it. . . . But they [the

Cainites] speak with impudence and blinded minds. For they make the devil akin to the master of all, the God of Jews and Christians and everyone, saying that he is the father of the devil's father, he who gave the law through Moses and worked so many wonders.[13]

In this passage we once again see a reference to a *Gospel of Judas* in the context of a discussion of the Cainites. Like the reference in Irenaeus's *Against Heresies*, this passage does not tell us who wrote it, when it was written, how many were in circulation, or if Epiphanius had even read it. While it seems likely that it is the same *Gospel of Judas* mentioned in Irenaeus's work, there is no way of knowing for sure (or if it was the same as the one recently discovered). It is also another passage that shows that there was disagreement among Cainites as to the motivation for Judas's actions.

What this passage does tell us, however, is that the *Gospel of Judas* contributed to the conviction that Judas was a hero, not a traitor. The Cainites esteemed many whom the orthodox saw as sinners and evil, and Judas, so it seems, had a special place in the Cainite sect as one who possessed the "highest knowledge." The *Gospel of Judas*, with its portrayal of Judas having a special meeting with Jesus, would have confirmed this conviction.

2. Why Did the *Gospel of Judas* Disappear?

We do not know when the *Gospel of Judas* "disappeared," but one way to measure when it did is by looking at when it was last referred to by others. After Epiphanius there is no more mention of a *Gospel of Judas*. What happened to the *Gospel of Judas* after the fourth century? Most likely the same thing that happened to other Gnostic texts. While there are some popular but baseless conspiracy theories regarding the elimination of Gnostic writings,[14] the demise of the *Gospel of Judas* and other such Gnos-

13. Epiphanius, *Panarion* 38, in *The Panarion of St. Epiphanius, Bishop of Salamis: Selected Passages* (New York: Oxford University Press, 1990), 133-35.

14. For one example, see Tom Harpur, *The Pagan Christ: Recovering the Lost Light* (To-

tic writings was most likely due to something much less spectacular. The following is a summary of some of the factors that would have collectively contributed to the disappearance of the document. It needs to be remembered that these factors would have equally applied to all Gnostic writings, not just the *Gospel of Judas*.

A. Formalizing of the Canon of Scripture

The term "canon" refers to those books that were eventually recognized by the church as authoritative for Christian belief and practice.[15] The process that eventually led to the formation of the New Testament canon began in the time of the first followers of Jesus. In response to the life-transforming message of Jesus, his followers began to write both about his life and to other Christians about the meaning of his life, death, and resurrection.

Paul was one of the first authors of books that later were canonized. His writings — which date from about A.D. 50 to just before his death in 65[16] — reflected his concern for his churches, and he interpreted the death and resurrection of Jesus for these Christians. He may have been involved in assembling the collection of his own letters — which were probably gathered together by the end of the first century in any case.[17]

ronto: Allen, 2004). For critiques of Harpur's book, see Gordon L. Heath, "Neither Scholarly Nor a Solution: A Response to Tom Harpur's *The Pagan Christ*," *McMaster Journal of Theology and Ministry* 6 (2005): 126-53; and Stanley E. Porter and Stephen J. Bedard, *Unmasking the Pagan Christ: An Evangelical Response to the Pagan Christ Idea* (Toronto: Clements, 2006).

15. For a helpful introduction to how the books of the Bible became a part of the canon, see David Ewert, *From Ancient Tablets to Modern Translations: A General Introduction to the Bible* (Grand Rapids: Zondervan, 1983); F. F. Bruce, *The Canon of Scripture* (Downers Grove: InterVarsity, 1988); Bruce M. Metzger, *The Early Versions of the New Testament* (London: Oxford University Press, 1975).

16. We recognize that some contend that some of Paul's letters are pseudepigraphal. However, even if this is the case (and we do not necessarily agree), the latest that one would date the Pastoral Epistles (1 and 2 Timothy, Titus) would be to the early years of the second century A.D.

17. On Paul's involvement in collecting his own letters and the formation of the Pau-

Other authors instead wrote accounts of Jesus' life, eventually called Gospels. The Gospels are anonymous works that are a form of Christian biography, written to depict the various events and sayings of Jesus. There may have been other early accounts of Jesus' life written, but the earliest one that we have is probably Mark's Gospel. Mark's Gospel was used by Matthew and Luke in the writing of their Gospels. Luke admits (1:1-4) that he was not the first to write about Jesus and that he had investigated what others had written when he wrote his account. Some would date Mark's Gospel to as early as around A.D. 45, while others would put it in the mid-60s, probably just before the Jewish War of 66-70. The other Gospels have been dated from sometime after Mark's up to around 85 or 90 at the latest. Usually John's Gospel is given the latest date of around 90. There may have been other sources that recorded sayings or deeds of Jesus, but none of these can rightly be called a Gospel.[18]

In the second century, there was increased Christian writing about the life of Jesus and about the lives of others associated with him. As a result, there was a wealth of Christian literature produced over the next few centuries. Some of this writing included accounts of Jesus that followed the canonical Gospels, while others related the "acts" of a variety of figures, and still others were letters to various churches. As this literature was being written, a process began whereby certain works began to emerge as the ones that were central to the life of the church. These works that began to emerge were selected according to their apostolic authorship, their doctrinal fidelity, and their attested usefulness in the early church.

As a result, it is in the second century that we have firm evidence that the canonical Gospels were given their titles. A number of scholars doubt that these titles have any bearing on authorship, but there are sub-

---

line canon, see Stanley E. Porter, "Paul and the Process of Canonization," in Craig A. Evans and Emanuel Tov, eds., *Exploring the Origins of the Bible* (Grand Rapids: Baker, in press).

18. The designation Q (from the German Word *Quelle,* "source") is often given to the sayings material that is shared by Matthew and Luke. Many think that this was a written source, while others believe it was simply oral tradition. In either form, it was not a gospel. The second-century *Gospel of Thomas* is a later pseudepigraphal work (and probably not even best called a gospel in the New Testament sense) and is discussed below.

stantial traditions that support the traditional authorship of these Gospels, including Mark as a follower of Jesus who got his account from Peter, possibly in Rome, Matthew as the tax collector and disciple, and Luke as the traveling companion of Paul. Whether the titles are accurate or not, by the second century we have significant evidence that the Gospels now in our canon were being joined together to form what is often called the fourfold Gospel. For example, we have a papyrus text with two of the Gospels in one manuscript (papyrus was an ancient form of paper made from the papyrus reed), Matthew and Luke (P4/64/67 [P indicates Papyrus]). In the middle part of the century, we have the heretic Marcion rejecting the other Gospels but only accepting Luke's and Tatian compiling his *Diatessaron* in 175, which was a composite account of the life and teaching of Jesus based upon our four canonical Gospels. By the end of the second and beginning of the third century, we have several codices with parts of more than one of the canonical Gospels (P75 with Luke and John; P45 with the Synoptic Gospels and Acts), and church fathers such as Irenaeus and others attesting to the four canonical Gospels. What is significant is that no other gospel is included with these canonical Gospels, indicating that already by this time the fourfold Gospel was established. We also have the bulk of the Pauline letters gathered in one document (P46 with Romans to 1 Thessalonians).[19] This process of gathering continued until the fourth century, when the solidified state of the canon is reflected in numerous comments and lists. The fourth century also saw the emergence of the major biblical codices. Codices (singular codex) are ancient books in the form of modern books rather than scrolls. These codices — the oldest complete Bibles that we possess — include essentially the same canon of books that we use today in our New Testament, apart from the occasional inclusion of a couple books that floated on the edge of the canon (for example, the *Epistle of Barnabas* and the *Shepherd of Hermas* in Codex Sinaiticus).

The formation of the canon was finalized and formalized in the

---

19. We must note that Hebrews is included in this collection of Pauline letters. It was a later inclusion in the canon and so occupied various places in the early days of canonical formation.

fourth century. The Council of Hippo in Africa (393) laid down the present New Testament as Scripture, and the twenty-seven books of the New Testament were decided upon — to the exclusion of all others. Various church councils that followed supported this selection of what books were "in" and what books were "out." Yet even before these councils, church leaders such as Athanasius (ca. 296-373), bishop of Alexandria, gave specific instructions on what books were considered apostolic (and thus authoritative). For instance, in his *Easter Letter* of 367, Athanasius sought to address the issue of "fabricated books" in circulation. In this letter, he outlined the present-day twenty-seven books of the New Testament as the canon, and then stated that

> these [books] are fountains of salvation, that they who thirst may be satisfied with the living words they contain. In these alone is proclaimed the doctrine of godliness. Let no man add to these, neither let him take aught from these.[20]

Athanasius went on in his letter to encourage the reading of other works such as the *Wisdom of Solomon,* the *Wisdom of Sirach,* and the *Shepherd of Hermas.* These books had been highly esteemed by Christians for a considerable amount of time, and were not considered to be Gnostic writings. But he made it clear that only the twenty-seven books of the New Testament belonged to the New Testament canon and were the standard of apostolic truth.

It must also be noted, however, that the canon was not formed in the fourth century, nor did Constantine have anything to do with the selection of texts for the New Testament (despite what Dan Brown says in *The Da Vinci Code*). For the most part, and with a few exceptions (none of the exceptions being among the four Gospels or Paul's letters), the canon was complete by the end of the second century.

As the fourth century progressed, nevertheless, it was clear that all Gnostic texts were officially "out." The Gnostic claims of special knowledge had been rejected, the true apostles' teaching was recognized and

20. Athanasius, *Letter 39,* in *Nicene and Post-Nicene Fathers, Second Series* 4 (Christian Literature, 1892; reprint, Peabody: Hendrickson, 2004).

formalized, and the church's future could be built on a firm and secure foundation.

B. Orthodox Christianity Becoming the Religion of the Empire

Christianity began the fourth century as a persecuted sect and ended the century as the official religion of the Roman Empire. The process of Christianization of the Roman Empire was long and painful and never a guaranteed thing. However, with the Roman Empire eventually adopting orthodox Christianity (orthodoxy defined by the decisions reached at the Council of Nicea, A.D. 325), there was little room for alternate Gnostic texts like the *Gospel of Judas*. In fact, Christian orthodoxy was increasingly a concern of the state, and this meant that alternative views had best be kept behind closed doors. That is not to say that church authorities automatically and joyfully became book-burning (and people-burning) fundamentalists, as sometimes portrayed. It is to say, however, that the social and religious milieu meant that it would be difficult for alternate texts to be copied and circulated.

C. Ignored by Scribes

In his summary of the history of the *Gospel of Judas*, Krosney provides a simple solution to explain its disappearance: scribes simply stopped copying it. He refers to the conclusion of David Brakke, who claims that the

> primary reason for the disappearance of these works is that scribes stopped copying them in antiquity and the Middle Ages. Professional scribes reproduced books by hand and only when a customer asked for a book and agreed to pay for it. If a Christian book was declared useless for theology and even dangerous, few people would order such books, and some scribes may have refused to supply them. Most of the manuscripts of Christian works that we have today were not produced by independent professional scribes, but in monasteries, and certainly monastic leaders would not authorize the copying of "heretical" books. Especially in antiquity, quality book materials and

scribal services were not cheap, so if there was no demand for a book, it could easily disappear.[21]

In other words, rather than look for a conspiracy, look at the many reasons that scribes would not have copied a document like the *Gospel of Judas*.

3. Conclusion

Based on this brief summary of the *Gospel of Judas* in early Christian writings, what can we say about the document's early history? First, the early Christian references to the gospel do not indicate who the author(s) was, when it was written (except it had to be written before ca. A.D. 180), or who were the original recipients.

Second, the references do indicate that the gospel was closely associated with the Cainites. The Cainites were mentioned at times without reference to the *Gospel of Judas*, but the *Gospel of Judas* was never mentioned without reference to the Cainites (both Irenaeus and Epiphanius comment on the *Gospel of Judas* in their discussion of the Cainites). This connection with the Cainites is noteworthy, for the recently discovered *Gospel of Judas* makes no mention of Cain. That it does not mention Cain or other "antiheroes from the Jewish Scriptures" as Irenaeus does leads Wurst to conjecture that there might have been more than one *Gospel of Judas* in circulation.[22] Meyer, however, argues that this lack of a reference to Cain does not necessarily mean that there were two gospels.[23] The lack of a reference to Cain or other anti-heroes does not seem to be critical, for the *Gospel of Judas* was obviously appreciated by the revisionist Cainites because it was a revisionist piece of literature and fit quite nicely into their approach to all biblical characters, not necessarily because it mentioned Cain.

21. As quoted in Herbert Krosney, *The Lost Gospel* (Washington: National Geographic, 2006), 202-3.

22. Wurst, "Irenaeus of Lyon," 126.

23. Marvin Meyer, "Judas and the Gnostic Connection," in Kasser, Meyer, and Wurst, eds., *The Gospel of Judas*, 137-69.

Third, the *Gospel of Judas* was the ultimate piece of radical revisionist literature. The sinners of the Old Testament (Cain, Seth, Sodomites) and the one who betrayed Jesus to the Roman authorities (Judas) were deemed by the Cainites and in the *Gospel of Judas* to be heroes. This radical rewriting of the Jewish and Christian story was understood to be contrary to the apostolic message as it had been received. As will be noted in Chapter Seven, this attempt to rehabilitate less-than-stellar or peripheral Bible figures is common in Gnostic literature.

Fourth, it is quite clear that the orthodox church leaders saw the Cainites as a heretical movement and the *Gospel of Judas,* which supported the Cainites, as a spurious and heretical document. The radical turning of the traditional biblical stories upside-down was considered completely unacceptable.

Fifth, the early Christian references do not tell us what happened to the *Gospel of Judas,* but they do provide clues. The rejection and eventual defeat of Gnosticism, the specific condemnations of the document, and the eventual triumph of orthodoxy in the fourth century and beyond meant that the chances of the *Gospel of Judas* (along with other heretical texts) surviving were quite slim.

CHAPTER FOUR

The Discovery of the *Gospel of Judas*
and Other Recent Finds

When the existence of the *Gospel of Judas* was first made widely known, some declared it the most important archaeological discovery in many years. They were no doubt thinking of it in relation to the earlier find of Coptic documents at Nag Hammadi, about 100 miles south of where the *Gospel of Judas* was purportedly discovered. The Nag Hammadi cache is significantly larger than the four manuscripts that include the *Gospel of Judas*. However, is it justified to say that this is the most important archaeological discovery in fifty years? A number of important archaeological finds have taken place in the course of the last 100 years. In fact, the twentieth century was one of incredible discoveries with direct relevance for study of the Bible, in particular the New Testament. A discussion of a few of these will help to put the *Gospel of Judas* in the context of other relatively recent discoveries. We will discuss four of them: ancient papyrus manuscripts, the Nag Hammadi Coptic library, the Dead Sea Scrolls, and some important ancient ossuaries.

1. Papyrus Manuscripts

The late nineteenth century and early twentieth century was an age of discovery of papyrus documents.[1] The term papyrus, which refers to the

---

1. On the papyri, including some of the most important recent discoveries, see

ancient form of paper made from the papyrus plant, is used in scholar-ship to refer more broadly to any number of materials on which ephem-eral documents were written. In contrast to inscriptions, which were written on permanent materials such as stone, papyri were written with-out the expectation of longevity. Materials used for such purposes in-clude not only papyrus, but parchment, bone, shards of pottery, and vari-ous other transient materials. However, climatic conditions in Egypt and some other places, such as Palestine, have made it possible for some such documents to survive their original temporary state. In the late nine-teenth century a number of significant finds of papyrus documents were made in Egypt. These discoveries came from what would have amounted to city garbage dumps, the material used in packing mummies, and the remains of ancient libraries. As a result, a huge number of papyrus docu-ments were discovered — estimates are that as many as several hundred thousand were discovered in a range of languages, especially Greek, but also Latin, Arabic, Coptic, and other languages. To date, probably only about a quarter to a half of all the discovered documents have been pub-lished, with many more discoveries to be gleaned from these artifacts. These documents included a wide range of important texts.

A. Chronicles of Everyday Life

Some of the papyri were documents that chronicled events in everyday life, such as wills, deeds, contracts, census reports, and receipts, among other things. Many of these were individual documents from now un-known people who were involved in a variety of forms of commerce. However, two very important collections of documents were discov-ered. One was the Zenon papyri.[2] Zenon was the administrator for a very important Egyptian landowner who held property in Egypt and

---

Roger S. Bagnall, *Reading Papyri, Writing Ancient History* (New York: Routledge, 1995); Stan-ley E. Porter, "Inscriptions and Papyri: Greco-Roman," in Craig A. Evans and Stanley E. Porter, eds., *Dictionary of New Testament Background* (Downers Grove: InterVarsity, 2000), 529-39.

2. See Rosalie R. E. Cook, "Zenon Papyri," in Evans and Porter, eds., *Dictionary of New Testament Background*, 1300-1303.

Palestine. The two thousand papyri in the Zenon collection document the correspondence between Zenon and various of his tenants over a variety of issues related to their farming endeavors. His description of the conditions of farming in the third century B.C. includes language that is in many instances reminiscent of Jesus' use of agricultural metaphors in his parables and helps to establish agricultural practices, economic conditions and personal relationships of the time. Another collection is the Babatha archive.[3] This is a collection of over thirty legal documents once belonging to a woman named Babatha. Babatha was a successful business woman, and these documents attest to her holdings. Babatha apparently fled from Nabatea, where she lived during the time of the Bar Kokhba revolt (A.D. 132-35) and hid out in a cave near the Dead Sea (now called the Cave of Letters, due to its finds). She apparently died in that cave and left her most important legal documents there. These documents attest to the kinds of transactions that she undertook, including the buying and selling of property. These also give insight into the particular restrictions on a woman in carrying out business transactions. All of these types of documents give insight into the socioeconomic context of the time of the New Testament. They illustrate social relations, give an idea of the nature and levels of business being transacted, and give insight into the economic climate of the times.

B. Literary Documents

A second type of papyrus document that has been discovered is literary texts. The rise of ancient scholarship took place around Alexandria in Egypt. As a result, numerous literary texts have been found in the rubbish heaps of ancient Egypt. These texts include a number of the known authors of the time, such as Homer, the Greek tragedians, and various poets and historians. Finding manuscripts of these various authors helps to establish the literary and reading priorities of those in the ancient world. Before the discovery of these papyri, often the earliest

---

3. See Stanley E. Porter, "Papyri, Palestinian," in Evans and Porter, eds., *Dictionary of New Testament Background*, 764-66, esp. 765-66.

manuscript for a given ancient author went back only to Byzantine or medieval times. With the discovery of these papyri, we now often have major manuscripts that go back even to Ptolemaic times (third and second centuries B.C.). These manuscripts often provide variant readings that help to assess and correct the texts of these ancient authors. Some of the literary manuscripts discovered are fragmentary, but a number of large and extensive manuscripts have been found as well. There have also been discoveries of a number of previously unknown authors or texts, and the rediscovery of works by authors whose writings disappeared. Examples of rediscovered works include Aristotle's *Athenian Constitution,* Bacchylides' poems, and plays of Menander among others. The Oxyrhynchus Historian is a writer whose account of the Peloponnesian war after Thucydides' account ends was discovered in the early years of the twentieth century. This document provides linguistic evidence regarding the type of Greek prose being written at the time and a historical account for an important episode in Greek history. There are a variety of other types of literary documents that have been found as well, including even ancient musical texts, among others.[4]

C. Religious Documents

A final category of papyrus documents to note is the semi-literary texts that include such works as apocryphal biblical texts and the copies of the New and Old Testaments. The first papyrus of the New Testament was published by the great biblical scholar and manuscript reader Constantin Tischendorf in 1868, the second in 1882 and 1885 by the early papyrologist Carl Wessely, and the third in 1892 by F. V. Scheil. All of the rest — and there are now about 120 papyri — have been published since 1898. Most were from Oxyrhynchus, but others were from a variety of places. There have been similar discoveries of the Old Testament in Greek. The earliest New Testament manuscript is a small portion of John 18 (P52 — the P stands for Papyrus) dated to around A.D. 125. Several major papyri to note

---

4. See Eric G. Turner, *Greek Papyri: An Introduction* (Oxford: Clarendon, 1968), esp. 97-100.

are P45, which contains major chunks of the four Gospels and Acts and is dated to the third century; P46, which contains most of Paul's letters (from Romans to 1 Thessalonians) and is dated to A.D. 200 at the latest; and P66, which contains a sizable portion of John's Gospel and is dated to the second century A.D. There have also been a number of apocryphal documents found, especially apocryphal gospels. The first was published in Vienna in 1885 (the Fayyum fragment), followed in 1897 by the first Greek fragments of what were later identified as the *Gospel of Thomas*. One of the most noteworthy discoveries was the *Egerton Gospel* papyrus (and P. Köln 255, which may be a part of it), published in 1935, which included a number of episodes about Jesus compiled from the Synoptic Gospels and John's Gospel. A number of other apocryphal texts have been published as well. The biblical manuscripts have clearly offered new readings of these biblical documents, and the apocryphal ones have offered further insight into the development of early Christian literature in response to what would later be called the canonical documents. As a point of comparison to the *Gospel of Judas,* it is worth noting that Comfort and Barrett have identified thirty-two papyri and parchment (animal skin used as a writing surface) documents of the New Testament that date from before A.D. 315, or around the time of the writing of the *Gospel of Judas,* including the much larger P45, P46, P66, and P75.[5]

A case can clearly be made that the discovery of the papyri constitutes a far more important set of discoveries than the *Gospel of Judas.* In fact, one should probably include the *Gospel of Judas* along with the other papyri that have been discovered — documents that continue to be found and published, adding insight into the ancient world, including the world of the New Testament.

2. Nag Hammadi Coptic Library

The Nag Hammadi Coptic library — mentioned elsewhere in this book, and its contents analyzed and commented upon as well — was discov-

5. Philip W. Comfort and David P. Barrett, *The Text of the Earliest New Testament Greek Manuscripts* (Wheaton: Tyndale, 2001).

ered in 1945 at the site of an ancient Egyptian monastery destroyed in the fourth century.[6] This collection of Coptic documents, consisting of twelve codices and some other leaves from a thirteenth codex, contains forty-five separate titles of works, some of them gospels. After some delays in publication of these documents, serious work began in the late 1960s, which translation work was soon sponsored by the Ministry of Culture of Egypt and UNESCO. The entire library was published by 1979. The works were published in Coptic editions and then in English translations (1977). One of the documents discovered was the Coptic *Gospel of Thomas*, which was one of the first documents published (1959).

The Nag Hammadi library of Coptic documents reflects Gnostic belief in many of its texts. All are thought to have been translated out of Greek and into Coptic, including the *Gospel of Thomas*, and the *Gospel of Mary* — although the earlier Greek text is no longer extant for the vast majority of these Coptic documents (P. Rylands III 463 may contain part of the *Gospel of Mary* in Greek). These Coptic Gnostic documents were found in jars probably stashed away around A.D. 400, when the monastery was destroyed. It is only one of several monasteries like this, however. In 1952, a Pachomian monastery (named after the Christian Pachomius, who founded the first Christian monastic order in the early fourth century) was found near Dishna (not far from Nag Hammadi). Apparently it was destroyed in the seventh century. This library had biblical, apocryphal, martyrological, and other theological texts, as well as a few fragments of secular authors mostly in Greek but also in Coptic.[7] The *Gospel of Judas* was found along with three other ancient documents in a single codex. Two of those texts — the *Letter of Peter to Philip* and the *First Revelation of James* — were nearly identical with those found at Nag Hammadi, and were probably part of a now lost Gnostic library with at least some similar contents to the one at Nag Hammadi.

Even within the perspective of the other Coptic finds, the *Gospel of*

6. On the discovery, see James M. Robinson, "Introduction," in Robinson, ed., *The Nag Hammadi Library in English* (San Francisco: Harper and Row, 1988), 22-26.

7. See James M. Robinson, *The Pachomian Monastic Library at the Chester Beatty Library and the Bibliotheque Bodmer* (ISAC Occasional Papers 19; Claremont: Claremont Graduate School, 1990).

Judas discovery is only of relative significance. It is clearly not the earliest Gnostic document, nor is it part of the largest set of Gnostic finds. Its lack of provenance makes it difficult to know how it helps our understanding of the world of fourth-century Coptic Christianity in Egypt.

3. The Dead Sea Scrolls

The Dead Sea Scrolls were discovered by chance in 1946 or 1947 when a shepherd boy tending his sheep threw stones into a cave near the Dead Sea and heard the shatter of pottery. Further exploration led to the discovery of eleven caves in which around 875 ancient documents had been stored, apparently by a group of people who had withdrawn from civilization to live in the desert near the Dead Sea.[8] This community lasted until the Romans swept through Palestine around A.D. 70. With the Roman onslaught upon them, those who lived at Qumran took their manuscripts and stashed them in caves so that they could preserve them and return to them later. For whatever reason, they never returned, and the documents remained there until they were discovered in the middle of the twentieth century. These documents were soon identified by scholars in Jerusalem and elsewhere as attesting to some of the earliest Hebrew manuscripts ever discovered. The Dead Sea Scrolls consist of a number of different types of documents.

A. Biblical Documents

Approximately 225 of the manuscripts discovered are simply biblical texts. One of the most important is the Great Isaiah Scroll. Previous to discovery of the Dead Sea Scrolls, the earliest manuscripts of the Hebrew Bible dated to early medieval times. With the discovery of the Dead Sea Scrolls the age of some of our biblical manuscripts was pushed back by a millennium.

8. See Michael O. Wise, "Dead Sea Scrolls: General Introduction," in Evans and Porter, eds., *Dictionary of New Testament Background*, 252-66.

B. Biblical Interpretative Documents

A second type of document is the biblical interpretative document. The Qumran community was probably an Essene community (one of the three "philosophies" identified by Josephus in describing the Jews of his time in the first century) that chose to live apart from society. Some Essenes lived in communities integrated with society, but those at Qumran apparently had rejected the priesthood in Jerusalem and lived apart. Some of their documents reveal their particular interpretation of Scripture. Their interpretation of Scripture focused upon their teacher of righteousness, who had established the community in opposition to the wicked priests of Jerusalem. Their form of biblical interpretation came to be known as the pesher method, in which they saw events depicted in Scripture as being fulfilled in their own time.

C. Sectarian Documents

A third type of document is sectarian documents designed for the community itself. There are a number of these, such as the Damascus Document, which contains historical material about the Qumran community and rules for their communal life; the Community Rule, which establishes and illustrates the standards of behavior to be followed by those in the community; the War Scroll, which is a set of guidelines for the eschatological war of the community against its enemies; and the like.

At the time of their discovery and first publication, the Dead Sea Scrolls aroused huge interest as they gave a new window into various forms of Judaism at the time of Jesus. In some instances, ways of interpreting Scripture by Jesus that seemed peculiar to him were seen to be mirrored by those at Qumran. Further, the kind of messianic consciousness that Jesus displayed was also seen to be present at Qumran. After the initial enthusiasm, there was a lag in the publication of the Qumran documents. In some ways, this only helped to fuel intrigue regarding what the rest of the Scrolls that had not been published contain. Finally, with the publication of the materials from Cave 4, most of the documents have been published, and have offered a wealth of materials to gain insights into the Judaism of the time and the world in which Jesus lived.

4. Significant Ossuaries

Throughout the twentieth century there were a number of significant discoveries of ossuaries, or ancient bone boxes, that offered insight into the world of the New Testament. As recounted by Craig Evans in his book on the topic, there were seven significant ossuary discoveries within the last century.[9] The first was the Nicanor ossuary, discovered in 1902. The Nicanor ossuary was one of seven discovered, but it had an inscription that stated that the bones were those of a son of Nicanor of Alexandria, "who built the doors."[10] This is one of several ossuaries of those involved in building in ancient Israel. This Nicanor may have been the builder of Nicanor's Gate referred to in rabbinic tradition (*b. Yoma* 19a). A second ossuary was that of Alexander son of Simon, discovered in 1941. There is some thought that this is the ossuary of Alexander, the son of Simon of Cyrene, mentioned in Mark 15:21. The Qorban ossuary was discovered in 1956. This ossuary has an inscription that is one of several inscriptions that have been discovered that attest to the practice mentioned in Mark 7:9-13. The house of David ossuary was discovered in 1971, which seems to indicate that in the time of Jesus there were some who believed that they could trace their ancestry back to David. The Caiaphas ossuary of 1990 contained the bones of a sixty-year-old man (along with others) and is thought perhaps to be the ossuary of the high priest Caiaphas (see Matthew 26:3, 57; Luke 3:2; John 11:49; 18:13, 14, 24, 28). Finally, there is the James ossuary of 2002. This ossuary had the words "James, son of Joseph, brother of Jesus" on it.[11] This ossuary con-

9. Craig A. Evans, *Jesus and the Ossuaries* (Waco: Baylor University Press, 2003), whose descriptions are followed here.

10. Evans, *Jesus and the Ossuaries*, 91.

11. Evans, *Jesus and the Ossuaries*, 112. Evans says that he takes no position on authenticity (p. 112), but by quoting extensively from William F. Albright (p. 118), he leaves the impression that he does believe it is probably authentic.

forms to the others in most respects, although the issue of uncertain provenance and some peculiarities with the paleography — to say nothing of what it says — have raised serious questions about its authenticity. Nevertheless, when this ossuary was discovered and made public, it aroused significant interest, as it seemed to provide substantiation for the New Testament account of the lineage of Jesus.[12]

It is arguable that almost any one of these ossuaries is at least as significant as the *Gospel of Judas,* because most of them provide first-hand evidence regarding the time surrounding the life and death of Jesus Christ.

5. Conclusion

All the excitement surrounding the unveiling of the *Gospel of Judas* should come as something of a surprise in the light of the other discoveries that have been made during this century. There is no doubt that the *Gospel of Judas* is of interest as one of the Gnostic documents of the third or fourth century. However, it and its companion documents are small by comparison with the other documents found at Nag Hammadi. There is also serious question whether the *Gospel of Judas* can in any way compete with many of the other discoveries made in the last one hundred years. The papyri finds uncovered a number of manuscripts of the New Testament itself — something from which the *Gospel of Judas* is several steps removed. The Dead Sea Scrolls have opened up new avenues of insight into the New Testament and Judaism by means of documents contemporary with the New Testament itself — something that the *Gospel of Judas* is several centuries away from. Even the ossuaries, even if they have not been as featured in the course of their discovery, offer brief glimpses not only into burial practice but into the lives and fortunes of some of the contemporaries of Jesus.

12. See the discussion in Hershel Shanks and Ben Witherington III, *The Brother of Jesus* (San Francisco: Harper, 2003), esp. 31-52.

CHAPTER FIVE

The Content of the
Gospel of Judas

The *Gospel of Judas* is a papyrus manuscript.[1] The manuscript was written on the ancient form of paper made from the special treatment of the papyrus plant. In ancient times, especially in the Mediterranean area, the papyrus plant was widely used as a reasonably abundant and affordable writing material. The plant was taken and cut into strips, and the strips were laid down in one direction, with another row on top placed perpendicular to the first. They were then pressed together and cured, so that the juices of the plant formed an adhesive. The side with the strips of plant running horizontally was considered the preferable side for writing, although writing was done on both sides. These pages were then gathered into what amounts to pages of a book. Like the Nag Hammadi Coptic library, the library of which the *Gospel of Judas* was a

1. The information on this manuscript is found in several places, including Rodolphe Kasser, Marvin Meyer, and Gregor Wurst, eds., *The Gospel of Judas from Codex Tchacos* (Washington: National Geographic, 2006), and Herbert Krosney, *The Lost Gospel: The Quest for the Gospel of Judas Iscariot* (Washington: National Geographic, 2006). We rely on their information. The English translation of the Gospel of Judas is found in Kasser, Meyer, and Wurst, with François Gaudard, "Gospel of Judas," in Kasser, Meyer, and Wurst, 19-45 (one notes that the English translators have included the divisions of the text to which we refer below). We have also used the Coptic text established by Rodolphe Kasser and Gregor Wurst, *The Gospel of Judas*, February 2006 and used for the English translation mentioned above and copyrighted by The National Geographic Society, April 2006.

part used the codex — or ancient form of book — to preserve and transmit their writings.[2]

This codex manuscript — greatly damaged over the years and requiring considerable restorative work — contains four Coptic documents. Two of them were already known from the Nag Hammadi Coptic library. They were the *Letter of Peter to Philip* (pages 1-9 of this codex, and found in codex 8 of the Nag Hammadi library) and the *First Revelation of James* (pages 10-32 of this codex, and found in codex 5 of the Nag Hammadi library). There is also an unknown document that has been severely damaged called the *Book of Allogenes* (pages 59-66 of this document; there are similar documents found at Nag Hammadi).[3]

The *Gospel of Judas* itself consists of thirteen sheets numbered on both sides (pages 33-58 of the codex), with writing on both sides, and so twenty-six pages of text written in Coptic. Although there has been damage to some of the pages, most of them are intact with twenty-five to twenty-nine lines of text on each page. Coptic was an ancient Egyptian language that originated in the late first or early second centuries and adapted the Greek alphabet, along with six letters from the ancient Egyptian Demotic language. Thus, the manuscript resembles a Greek manuscript, even though it is in a different language. Nevertheless, because of the influence of Greek as the trade language of the ancient Greco-Roman world, there were a number of Greek loan words that were used in Coptic. The use of loan words was enhanced by missionary efforts to reach the Egyptian population through Coptic, which resulted early on in the Bible being translated into Coptic.[4]

The *Gospel of Judas* is apparently a complete literary work, opening with an introduction and closing with a postscript. The document has many of the features of both typical Coptic Gnostic literature and New Testament literature. The work is called a "gospel" because it calls itself a gospel. The *Gospel of Judas* concludes with the words "Gospel of Judas." In

---

2. On papyrus and the codex, see Eric G. Turner, *Greek Papyri: An Introduction* (Oxford: Clarendon, 1968), 2-16.

3. All of these works are found in James M. Robinson, ed., *The Nag Hammadi Library in English* (San Francisco: Harper and Row, 1988), including an *Allogenes* (pp. 490-500).

4. See C. C. Walters, *An Elementary Coptic Grammar* (Oxford: Blackwell, 1976), iii-iv.

this way it is not like the New Testament Gospels — none of which has a title or author mentioned — but it resembles other Gnostic gospels, such as the *Gospel of Thomas*, which concludes with an explicit postscript. Unlike the *Gospel of Thomas*, however, as the editors note, the *Gospel of Judas* does not say "gospel according to Judas," identifying Judas as the author, but that it is a gospel about Judas.[5] Thus, this gospel makes no claim to being from Judas, only being about him.

The *Gospel of Judas* begins with an "Introduction: Incipit" that states that it is a secret document revealing material spoken between Jesus and Judas Iscariot in conversation before the last supper. This opening places the *Gospel of Judas* within the scope of other Gnostic literature that emphasizes special revelation of secret knowledge to those who are within the boundaries of the group. This opening distinguishes the *Gospel of Judas* from the New Testament Gospels, however, because they have a much wider scope — the New Testament Gospels cover the period of Jesus' entire ministry as a minimum — and they include both dialogue and narrative, whereas this is simply a dialogue. A distinction is sometimes made by scholars between narrative and sayings gospels. If this distinction holds, then the *Gospel of Judas* is clearly a sayings gospel, unlike the New Testament Gospels, which are all narrative gospels. However, this distinction is highly questionable. Later writers have sometimes entitled their collections of sayings and dialogues as gospels (e.g., the *Gospel of Thomas*), but there is no indication that the earliest gospels were anything other than narrative gospels.

Although the *Gospel of Judas* itself does not contain division headings, the manuscript itself is divided into sub-units. There is, for example, a small space that separates what is called the "Introduction: Incipit" from the subsequent material. The opening is followed by a general description of Jesus' earthly ministry as one during which he "performed miracles" and did "great wonders," as well as calling twelve disciples. To these disciples, it says, he chose to reveal mysteries regarding "what would take place at the end," presumably the end of time although this might refer to the end of his life. It also says that he appeared to his disci-

5. Kasser, Meyer, and Wurst, with Gaudard, "Gospel of Judas," 45 n. 151.

ples as a child, reminiscent of some of the material in the infancy gospels found at Nag Hammadi.

The translators and editors of the *Gospel of Judas* have divided the content of the gospel into three major scenes, each with two or more sub-scenes. As noted above, these units and sub-units (though not the headings) are often indicated in the manuscript by small spaces or other indicators such as paragraph markers.

Scene one involves a thanksgiving prayer over the bread at what is clearly a eucharistic service. The editors divide this scene into three sub-units. This is not a depiction of the last supper, although there are similarities, but a depiction of a later formalized eucharistic service. After the participants are seated and Jesus has offered a thanksgiving prayer, he laughs. When the disciples ask about this, he insists that he is not laughing at them but that through this "your god" will be praised. The disciples insist that Jesus is their god. Jesus then states that people of this generation (as opposed to earlier generations) will not know him. The editors believe that "your god" is a reference to "the ruler of this world," not the God above.[6]

At this, in the second sub-unit, the disciples become angry and, the text says, blaspheme in their hearts. When Jesus confronts them over this to produce the perfect human who can stand before him, the only one who comes forward is Judas Iscariot. Judas acknowledges Jesus as from the aeon (or divine emanation) of Barbelo,[7] but admits that he is not worthy to state the name of the one who sent Jesus.

---

6. Kasser, Meyer, and Wurst, with Gaudard, "Gospel of Judas," 21 n. 13.

7. The editors note that Barbelo is used in Sethian Gnostic texts of "the divine Mother of all, who often is said to be the Forethought *(pronoia)* of the Father, the infinite One. The name of Barbelo seems to be based on a form of the tetragrammaton. . . ." Kasser, Meyer, and Wurst, with Gaudard, "Gospel of Judas," 23 n. 22. For more on Barbelo, who is often associated with Sophia (wisdom), see Hans Jonas, *The Gnostic Religion: The Message of the Alien God and the Beginnings of Christianity* (second ed.; Boston: Beacon, 1963), 199-200; Kurt Rudolph, *Gnosis: The Nature and History of Gnosticism* (trans. Robin McL. Wilson; San Francisco: Harper, 1987), 80-81; Meyer, "Judas and the Gnostic Connection," in Kasser, Meyer, and Wurst, eds., *Gospel of Judas,* 143-57. Barbelo is especially associated with the Gnostic thought found in the *Apocryphon of John* (see Frederik Wisse, "The Apocryphon of John," in Robinson, ed., *Nag Hammadi Library,* 104-23).

In the third sub-unit, Jesus and Judas then step aside to speak privately about the mysteries of God's reign. Jesus speaks to Judas of someone being chosen to replace him, an apparent reference to Judas being replaced after his betrayal of Jesus by Matthias in Acts 1:15-26.[8] Judas is interested in when this revelation of insight, called a "great day of light," will come, but Jesus suddenly leaves.

Scene two is divided into four sub-units by the editors and again concerned with Jesus' appearance to his disciples. The disciples are interested in where he went. Jesus says that he has gone to another generation, which he calls "great" and "holy." The disciples inquire about this generation, and again Jesus laughs. He tells them that no one of this generation or aeon[9] will have any part of that generation, apparently drawing a contrast between the spiritual generation and the earthly generation and how they will never intersect.

Reminiscent of Mark 13 and its parallels (Matthew 24 and Luke 21:5-36), in the second sub-unit, the disciples observe that they have seen a temple with people, priests, and an altar. When Jesus asks what they are like, the disciples describe them as immoral and perverted, though acting in Jesus' name. This is probably a reference to enemies of the Gnostics.[10]

Jesus then offers an allegorical interpretation of the temple episode in the next sub-unit, in which he links those who serve in the temple to the god of this world. Each of their actions has symbolic significance.[11] This allegory is typical of Gnostic interpretation and found throughout the *Gospel of Judas*. Jesus concludes by saying that in the end these evildoers will be put to shame. The rest of the section is fragmentary, but indicates that their opponents will eventually be overcome.

8. See Kasser, Meyer, and Wurst, with Gaudard, "Gospel of Judas," 23 n. 25.

9. On the aeons, see Kasser, Meyer, and Wurst, with Gaudard, "Gospel of Judas," 24 n. 31. See also Rudolph, *Gnosis,* 67-69.

10. The editors take it as the "leaders of the emerging orthodox Church." Kasser, Meyer, and Wurst, with Gaudard, "Gospel of Judas," 26 n. 40. See our Chapter Nine, below.

11. The editors interpret the scene as a "Metaphor for erroneous religious instruction, apparently in the emerging orthodox Church. The priests are the disciples, and perhaps their successors in the Church, and the animals led to the slaughter are the victims of the improper religious observance in the church." See Kasser, Meyer, and Wurst, with Gaudard, "Gospel of Judas," 27 n. 46.

In the final sub-unit of this scene, Judas asks Jesus about that generation. Jesus says that every human dies, but that those of that generation
will live and be taken up. The others, however, are like seed sown on
rocky ground and they produce nothing, an allusion to the parable of
the sower (Matthew 13:3-23; Mark 4:1-20; Luke 8:4-15).

Scene three is divided into ten sub-units and is concerned with Judas
retelling a vision he has had to Jesus and Jesus' response to him. Judas
approaches Jesus about this "great vision," but Jesus greets him with
laughter and asks why Judas, the thirteenth spirit (as the editors say, "the
disciple excluded from the circle of the twelve"),[12] is so determined to
find out everything. Judas then relates his vision, in which the twelve disciples stone him and persecute him. He further sees a house with a green
roof. Jesus tells Judas that he has been misled, and that no mortal is per-
mitted to enter that house, only the holy. Jesus concludes by telling Judas
that he has explained "the mysteries of the kingdom" to him.

Judas asks in the next sub-unit whether he is under the spiritual control of the rulers of the earthly sphere. When Jesus says that he will
grieve when he sees the kingdom, Judas expresses dismay regarding why
he has been allowed to see this if he is designated for that generation. Jesus clarifies that he is to be the thirteenth disciple and cursed by the others, even though he will eventually be elevated to the holy level.

In the next several sub-units, various Gnostic teachings are laid out
through the mouth of Jesus. In the first of these, Jesus takes Judas aside
to teach him secrets hidden from other humans. These secrets are concerned with the realms beyond this earth. In this world, an angel called
Self-Generated emerges who is the creator of all other things.

Adam,[13] Judas is then told in the next sub-unit, is one of the first
things created in the luminous world, and he is joined by many others,
including the generation of his son Seth and his descendants.[14] Jesus

12. Kasser, Meyer, and Wurst, with Gaudard, "Gospel of Judas," 31 n. 74.

13. The name is "Adamas," but it represents Adam, the first human, seen here "as in
many other gnostic texts, to be the paradigmatic human of the divine realm and the exalted image of humanity." Kasser, Meyer, and Wurst, with Gaudard, "Gospel of Judas," 35
n. 100. On Gnostic anthropology, see Rudolph, *Gnosis*, 86-113.

14. On Seth as a redemption or savior figure of the human race in Gnosticism, see

goes into detail on the various aeons and heavens and their organization. This is a complex hierarchy of heavenly beings. Gnostic cosmology revolves around separation between the heavenly and earthly realms, mediated by a number of intermediate figures, such as aeons, spirits, and the like. The cosmos is subject to decay, but it is in the cosmos that the "first human" appeared. There is one aeon that appeared with this generation, and its name is El, the ancient Semitic name for God. Other names used of such beings are Nebro, Yaldabaoth (Ialdabaoth), and Saklas.[15] The next sub-unit says there are twelve rulers and gives the names of five. The first is Seth who is "called Christ."[16]

The creation of humanity, depicted in the next sub-unit, is directly dependent upon the account in Genesis 1. In fact, the two humans are called Adam and Eve, although Eve is also known by the name Zoe. They are told that they will live a long time. Judas then in the next sub-unit inquires about the destiny of Adam and the rest of humanity. Jesus asks regarding his curiosity and clarifies that the reason humans were given divine spirits is so that they might help God. In fact, Jesus goes further in the next sub-unit and states that God gave Adam and others knowledge (*gnōsis*) so that those of the world — those of chaos and the underworld — will not be able to have control over them. For all of them, Jesus insists, there will be an end to all of the stars, who act immorally.

In the last sub-unit, Judas inquires regarding those who have been baptized. Jesus apparently answers affirmatively toward baptism (although the language is fragmentary at this point). More than that, Jesus commends Judas as one who will excel beyond any other. The reason is that Judas "will sacrifice the man that clothes" Jesus, that is, help him to sacrifice his earthly body and thereby liberate his soul from it. With this,

---

Rudolph, *Gnosis*, 131-40; Meyer, "Judas and the Gnostic Connection," in Kasser, Meyer, and Wurst, eds., *Gospel of Judas*, 157-66.

15. On various of these cosmological figures, see Kasser, Meyer, and Wurst, with Gaudard, "Gospel of Judas," 36-38 notes 106-115. These figures are also discussed in Rudolph, *Gnosis*, passim, and Jonas, *Gnostic Religion, passim*.

16. The editors note that "Christ is described as the manifestation of Seth in this world" in Christian Sethian Gnostic documents. See Kasser, Meyer, and Wurst, with Gaudard, "Gospel of Judas," 38 n. 116; Meyer, "Judas and the Gnostic Connection," 166-69.

Jesus tells Judas that he has been told everything, and that he should keep his eye on a particular star that will guide him. When he lifts his head, Judas sees a "luminous cloud" and hears a voice from heaven in his own transfiguration scene (cf. Matthew 17:1-8; Mark 9:2-8; Luke 9:28-36).

The conclusion to the gospel, entitled "Judas betrays Jesus," includes the high priests grumbling because Jesus has gone away for prayer. The leaders are watching for the right moment to arrest Jesus. However, his popularity with the people has made the religious leaders afraid. When Judas approaches them, they are curious regarding his presence, and he is paid money for handing over Jesus. As noted above, the manuscript ends with the words "Gospel of Judas."

CHAPTER SIX

The Authenticity of the
Gospel of Judas

A manuscript such as the *Gospel of Judas* is a complex artifact that combines a number of different elements together. Therefore, the question of the authenticity of this manuscript entails a number of different questions. Are we questioning the authenticity of the actual manuscript, or the story that it contains, or what exactly? We will attempt to answer this question in terms of three questions.

1. Is the Manuscript a Modern Forgery?

One of the first questions to ask regarding a manuscript such as this is whether it is a modern forgery. There have been numerous modern forgeries foisted upon the scholarly world, including some possibly related to biblical studies. We unfortunately do not know or recognize the forgeries that have not been discovered. We are only aware of those that we have unmasked. Two finds that have been suspected of being forgeries are the so-called *Secret Gospel of Mark*, supposedly found by Morton Smith, and the James ossuary. The *Secret Gospel of Mark* is a supposed alternative version of Mark's Gospel found by Smith in 1958 at Mar Saba Monastery embedded in a letter purportedly by Clement of Alexandria and written on the endpapers of a seventeenth-century edition of

Ignatius's letters.[1] The James ossuary is an ossuary or ancient bone box used for reburial of the bones of the dead with an inscription that said "James, son of Joseph, brother of Jesus." Later research has shown that there is a high probability that the *Secret Gospel of Mark* was forged by Morton Smith, while there is still dispute over the James ossuary (see Chapter Four for brief discussion of this and other ossuaries).

The fact that a supposedly ancient document utilizes old materials is not proof that it is not a modern forgery, as the best forgers use old materials. For example, they use the kind of writing instruments, inks, and papers that the ancients would have used. Another factor to consider is the provenance of an ancient discovery. Because of forgeries of ancient artifacts, as well as the tendency for thievery of ancient artifacts to occur, modern archaeologists desire to be able to establish the pedigree of an ancient artifact. In other words, they like to be able to establish the chain of custody from first discovery at the archaeological site up to contemporary possession. Here the *Gospel of Judas* runs into some trouble.

Herbert Krosney has given an account of the purported discovery of the manuscript. According to one account, the manuscript was found sometime in the 1970s in a network of catacombs at a place northeast of Al Minya, called Jebel Qarara.[2] However, more recent efforts to find this same cave resulted in reports of the actual site being up to about five miles away.[3] As a result, Krosney concludes that the "manuscript's early trail has now gone cold."[4] The story picks up again when the manuscript is in the possession of an Egyptian antiquities dealer by the name of Hanna Asabil (a pseudonym). As Krosney reports, however, Hanna offered several different stories of how he came to possess the manuscript. One is that he inherited the manuscript from his father and from his father before him for several generations. A variation on this story indicates that the manuscript passed into the father's hands right after

1. See S. C. Carlson, *The Gospel Hoax: Morton Smith's Invention of Secret Mark* (Waco: Baylor University Press, 2005).

2. Herbert Krosney, *The Lost Gospel: The Quest for the Gospel of Judas Iscariot* (Washington: National Geographic, 2006), 22-24.

3. Krosney, *The Lost Gospel*, 25-27.

4. Krosney, *The Lost Gospel*, 27.

World War II (to avoid difficulties with Egyptian laws passed in 1951 regulating the antiquities trade). A second story is an account similar to the account regarding the Nag Hammadi documents. Supposedly farmers were plowing and the ground fell away and they found themselves inside a tomb, where the manuscript was found alongside a mummy.[5] Despite the lack of clear provenance, however, on the basis of the reports from those who have seen the manuscript and been involved in its preservation and restoration, it appears that the manuscript was probably discovered at an ancient site, even if that site is not now known or accessible. The nature of the document itself — in terms of not only the papyrus and ink, but the language used on it — indicates that those who were responsible for possessing and transmitting it in modern times were almost assuredly not involved in creating it.

2. Is the Manuscript an Ancient Document and How Old Is It?

If the document is not a modern forgery, then the question is whether it is an ancient document, and if an ancient document how old it might be. There are a number of tests that can be done to determine its age. One is to test the age of the materials that it is made of. This would indicate a date before which it cannot be created. Another is to investigate comparative historical data, such as its similarities to other documents and its ideas, ancient references, and the like, to place it in an appropriate environment.

In so far as the materials are concerned, the manuscript has the appearance of age. Apparently, when Rodolphe Kasser, the expert in Coptic (known as a Coptologist) who was instrumental in reconstructing the document and translating it, first examined the manuscript, he dated it to the fourth century A.D.[6] He determined this on the basis of the material used in its writing — the papyrus and the ink — and the paleography, that is, the style and type of ancient handwriting that was used. Papyrus

5. Krosney, *The Lost Gospel*, 31.
6. Krosney, *The Lost Gospel*, 274.

was used as the paper of the ancient world for over a millennium, so the fact that papyrus is used does not establish the date. The ink that is used on the manuscript is apparently what is called an iron gall ink, in which the carbon-based ink is mixed with gum and iron.[7] This helps to narrow down the date, but probably only to within a few centuries, such as from the third to the seventh centuries. Comparison of the handwriting with other scripts perhaps helps to narrow down the time-frame a little further, but the dating of handwriting is notoriously imprecise.

The notoriety that is attached to this manuscript has resulted in its being studied by radiocarbon dating. Krosney records the account of the initial unveiling of the manuscript, at which time an expert in carbon-14 dating was present. He was able to take with him five pieces of papyrus (one with leather attached from the cover) and subject them to carbon-14 dating. The two pieces of papyrus from the manuscript itself gave a date of A.D. 279, give or take 47 or 50 years; a piece from the inside of the outside cover, 209, give or take 58 years; the piece of leather and attached papyrus, 223, give or take 51 years. One piece of loose papyrus indicated A.D. 333, give or take 48 years. As a result, the expert in carbon-14 dating concluded with 95% confidence that the leather binding and papyrus of the manuscript dated to a range of A.D. 220 to 340.[8] Similarly, tests on the ink indicate that it is consistent with an ink being used in the third century A.D. The date of the materials indicates a date before which the manuscript could not have been written. In other words, the dating of the papyrus indicates that it dates to A.D. 220 to 340 or after, but not before. The mean age has been calculated at A.D. 280.[9] There is another interesting point to note, however. The *Gospel of Judas* was found along with several other documents. One of these is a mathematical treatise that designates its origins in an area called Pagus 6. This refers to an area in the Oxyrhynchite Nome that apparently only came into being in A.D. 307 or 308. If these manuscripts had common origins — this is not certain, but they were apparently discovered together and always traveled together

7. Krosney, *The Lost Gospel*, 304.
8. Krosney, *The Lost Gospel*, 272-73.
9. Krosney, *The Lost Gospel*, 275.

until around 2001 — then this may well indicate a date of sometime after 307 or 308 for the origination of this manuscript of the *Gospel of Judas*.[10]

The comparative data support the notion that the manuscript was written in the third to fourth century along several lines. One is the fact that the handwriting used is, according to one Coptologist, in a hand very similar, but not identical in any given instance, to the Coptic hand found in the Nag Hammadi documents.[11] The Nag Hammadi documents were the single largest find of Coptic documents. Forty-five different documents were found in thirteen codices. The Nag Hammadi find was discovered about 100 miles south of where the *Gospel of Judas* and the other documents were found and has been dated roughly to the middle of the fourth century A.D. The content of the *Gospel of Judas* is consistent with the kinds of documents found at Nag Hammadi, reflects a highly consistently similar Gnostic worldview, and is consistent with ancient references, such as those found in Irenaeus and Epiphanius, to Gnostic writings of the time.[12] Some of the most obvious Gnostic features of the *Gospel of Judas* include reference to Barbelo, Seth, aeons, angels, spirits, and private knowledge, among many others.

Consequently, a reasonable conclusion is that this particular manuscript of the *Gospel of Judas* was written by Gnostics as part of the Gnostic movement in Egypt sometime in the early to mid part of the fourth century A.D.

3. Is the Coptic Manuscript a Later Version of an Earlier Greek Document?

In the middle of his discussion of the initial confrontation of three experts with the *Gospel of Judas*, including an early church historian, a

---

10. Krosney, *The Lost Gospel*, 298. Cf. p. 222 for description of when the mathematical treatise was separated from the other documents.

11. Krosney, *The Lost Gospel*, 303.

12. Each of these is discussed elsewhere in this book, including Chapter Four on the Nag Hammadi finds, Chapter Two on Gnosticism and its beliefs, and Chapter Three on early church references.

Coptologist, and a carbon-14 expert, Krosney concludes that "It was almost definitely a Coptic translation from an early document written in Greek, probably one dating from the second or third century. Many Gnostic documents stemmed from that period."[13] An assumption of Coptic studies today is that most if not all our later Coptic manuscripts, including those found at Nag Hammadi, are translations from earlier Greek. Even though the Greek manuscript evidence for this is very slight, scholars believe that this is the case on the basis of what Greek evidence there is, citations in early Greek church fathers, and other descriptions and summaries by early Greek authors.[14] Examples of extant Greek documents of later Coptic texts include the Greek *Gospel of Thomas* fragments from the second or third centuries, a Greek manuscript of the *Acts of Thomas,* and a possible fragment from the *Gospel of Mary.* A portion of Plato's *Republic* and some of the *Sentences of Sextus* in Coptic were also found at Nag Hammadi.

The best-known example is the Coptic *Gospel of Thomas.* The complete Coptic *Gospel of Thomas* was discovered at Nag Hammadi and was the first of the Coptic documents to be published (1959). It contains a series of sayings attributed to Jesus but purportedly recorded by Thomas. In the late nineteenth and early twentieth centuries, three fragments of what seemed to be previously unknown sayings of Jesus in Greek were discovered (these are the so-called *Oxyrhynchus Logia of Jesus* and subsequent finds, P.Oxy. 1, 654, and 655). It was only later that they were able to be identified as an earlier Greek source from the second century of the *Gospel of Thomas.* Most of the works discovered at Nag Hammadi, however, do not have an earlier Greek version for comparison.

It may well be that the recently discovered *Gospel of Judas* is a translation from Greek, but we do not know when that original was written or what that earlier Greek version may have looked like. The parallels between the *Gospel of Judas* and the *Gospel of Thomas* are not conclusive either, as there are a number of differences between the two. The *Gospel of*

13. Krosney, *The Lost Gospel,* 267.
14. See Bentley Layton, *The Gnostic Scriptures* (Garden City: Doubleday, 1987), xxiii-xxv.

Thomas is a pseudepigraphal sayings source that claims to record sayings that Thomas himself heard from Jesus. The *Gospel of Judas* is not a book by Judas but a book about Judas. There is no claim to authorship by a disciple. Thus, even if the *Gospel of Judas* is a translation from an earlier Greek original, we do not know when that document was written, when it was translated, or what its specific contents were. The authenticity of an earlier Greek version cannot be established to the same degree of certainty as can the fourth-century date of the extant Coptic document.

4. Conclusion

Authenticity is a potentially slippery subject, as it can mean a number of different things. The provenance of the *Gospel of Judas* is suspect, but what little we do know indicates that the document is probably not a modern forgery. There is little doubt that the *Gospel of Judas* appears to be an ancient artifact, probably written some time between A.D. 300 and 350. The physical features of the papyrus, its ink, and the paleography indicate this, the ideas it contains are consonant with ancient Gnostic thought of the time, and the date is confirmed by scientific testing by the carbon-14 method. It may even be probable that the recently discovered *Gospel of Judas* is the one Irenaeus referred to. However, we cannot establish that to the same degree of certainty as we can establish its being an ancient document from the fourth century, since we cannot establish when the document mentioned by Irenaeus would have been written, when it would have been translated, or what it would have specifically contained.

CHAPTER SEVEN

Rehabilitation Literature
of the Gnostics

Gnosticism was not mainstream Christianity.[1] It was on the outer fringes of Christianity and hence aroused the ire of those in the mainstream such as Irenaeus and Epiphanius. There were many things that characterized Gnosticism in their beliefs and practices.[2] As we discuss elsewhere, Gnostics had a particular set of beliefs that revolved around secret knowledge, a complex cosmogony and cosmology in which the earthly and the heavenly were divided and mediated only by divine emanations, and a view of humanity that required salvation through redemptive figures and procedures. They also had their own particular practices that governed their life in community, which had the effect of distancing them from mainstream Christian religious life. This eventually came to an end for a variety of reasons, anywhere from the end of the fourth to the eighth centuries. Perhaps as an understandable response to the situation in which they found themselves — theologically marginalized and isolated in their practices — the Gnostics also took on a different perspective toward the biblical figures, which they reflected in their own writings. As was noted above in discussion of the Nag Hammadi library, the Gnostics wrote a significant amount of their own literature, geared toward explaining and

1. We discuss the question of orthodoxy and heresy in Chapter Nine.
2. For a summary, see Chapter Two, and Kurt Rudolph, *Gnosis: The Nature and History of Gnosticism* (trans. Robin McL. Wilson; San Francisco: Harper, 1987), 53-272.

defending their particular marginalized worldview. One of the characteristics of this literature is that it is what might best be called rehabilitation literature. By rehabilitation literature, we mean that the Gnostics wrote a form of literature that attempted to take marginalized and tangential figures in the Old and New Testaments and place them at the center of religious belief and function. This reflects the perspective in which the Gnostics saw themselves — as marginalized people who were attempting to find a way to the center of belief. They were never able to do this in so far as Christianity was concerned. Nevertheless, this did not prevent them from attempting to do so by offering an apologetic on behalf of others in the biblical text who had found themselves similarly marginalized. As we noted in Chapter Two, some of the Old Testament figures who are rehabilitated are Cain, Seth, and the Sodomites. The *Gospel of Judas* is one of these pieces of rehabilitation literature as well.

In this chapter, we wish to offer several other examples of rehabilitation literature using New Testament figures, as a way of showing how the Gnostics approached the issue of marginalization, and thereby helping to account for what we find in the *Gospel of Judas* as an attempt to rehabilitate the figure of Judas Iscariot from betrayer and traitor to befriender and helper.

1. Gospels of the Marginalized

As we noted in Chapter Two, there are a number of gospels found within the Nag Hammadi Coptic literature. These gospels attempt to promote and centralize characters who are marginal to the biblical account as a part of the apologetic stance of Gnosticism in its attempt to make itself theologically central. In fact, the three of the four gospels that are attributed to individuals in the Gnostic library constitute this kind of literature.

A. The *Gospel of Thomas*

The disciple Thomas appears in only a limited number of places in the New Testament. In five places he is referred to simply in the lists of disciples: Matthew 10:3; Mark 3:18; Luke 6:15; John 21:2; and Acts 1:13. It is only in John's Gospel that Thomas has a relatively larger role. In two places, Thomas speaks: "Thomas, called the Twin, said to his fellow disciples, 'Let us also go, that we may die with him'" (John 11:16); and "Thomas said to him, 'Lord, we do not know where you are going; how can we know the way?'" (John 14:5). In only one instance does Thomas play any significant role in the canonical Gospel narratives. In John 20, Thomas is not present when Jesus appears to the disciples and says that he will not believe unless he sees explicit evidence (vv. 24-25). Eight days later, Jesus appears to him (v. 26) and asks him to put his finger in his hands and side (v. 27), at which point Thomas believes (v. 28). The scene of belief is moving, but it is not an action that is commended. Jesus expresses surprise at Thomas's belief and rebukes him by saying that those are blessed who believe without having to have such evidence presented to them (v. 29). In other words, Thomas is not a model to emulate.

Thomas is therefore a good candidate for rehabilitation by the Gnostics. There is something known about him, but he is clearly on the margins of the New Testament account. He is a doubting disciple, one who is of but not in the group. The fact that the Gnostics use a character from John's Gospel is even more poignant. John's Gospel is sometimes linked to Gnostic thought in the sense that it posits a world that seems to know the kinds of oppositions and dualisms of Gnosticism, but it overcomes them by seeing a genuine and true mediation between God and humanity through the incarnate Jesus Christ.[3] Nevertheless, the Gnostics created the *Gospel of Thomas*.[4]

---

3. See Craig S. Keener, *The Gospel of John: A Commentary* (2 vols.; Peabody: Hendrickson, 2003), 1:161-69.

4. There have been some, especially those associated with the Jesus Seminar, who wish to date the *Gospel of Thomas* to among the earliest Christian documents, giving it priority along with the canonical Gospels. See, e.g., Robert W. Funk, Roy W. Hoover, and The Jesus Seminar, *The Five Gospels* (New York: Macmillan, 1993). Most scholars believe that the *Gospel of Thomas* is later and derivative from the Synoptic Gospels. See, e.g., James H. Charlesworth and Craig A. Evans, "Jesus in the Agrapha and Apocryphal Gospels," in Bruce Chilton and Craig A. Evans, eds., *Studying the Historical Jesus* (Leiden: Brill, 1994), 496-503, esp. 497. The latest research posits a variation of this latter position — that the *Gospel of Thomas* was dependent on Tatian's *Diatessaron*, a harmony of the Gospels

The gospel contains a number of references to Thomas that are worth mentioning.[5] It opens by saying that the book contains "secret sayings" that Jesus spoke and that Didymos Judas Thomas wrote and closes by saying that this is the "Gospel according to Thomas." The opening and closing are ways in which the Gnostics seem to be saying that Thomas was one of the insiders, to whom Jesus himself would entrust his very words. He has moved from the position of doubting outsider to trusted insider and recorder. This is confirmed by one scene in the series of sayings within the gospel. In saying 13, reminiscent of the disciples' confession in Mark 8:27-29 (cf. Matthew 16:13-16; Luke 9:18-20), Jesus asks the disciples to compare him to someone. Simon Peter says Jesus is like a righteous angel, Matthew says that he is like a wise philosopher. Thomas admits being "wholly incapable of saying whom you are like." We see here that now Thomas has been elevated to the inner circle of disciples whom Jesus asks for their opinions. The climactic opinion is uttered by Thomas — although he is still speechless.

B. The *Gospel of Philip*

There are two Philips in the New Testament, one a disciple of Jesus and the other one of the seven chosen to work with Stephen who later evangelizes the Ethiopian eunuch in Acts 8:26-40. Philip the disciple is the one who is probably meant, because his authorship is attached to a gospel that contains some reference to Jesus.[6] It is the other Philip who plays a larger role in the New Testament. The references to Philip the disciple occur in two different places. One is the lists of disciples found in Matthew 10:3; Mark 3:18; Luke 6:14; and Acts 1:13. There are four other incidents in the Gospels involving Philip, all in John's Gospel. In John 1, Jesus

---

written in A.D. 175. See Nicholas Perrin, *Thomas and Tatian: The Relationship between the Gospel of Thomas and the Diatessaron* (Leiden: Brill, 2002).

5. See Helmut Koester and Thomas O. Lambdin, "The Gospel of Thomas," in James M. Robinson, ed., *The Nag Hammadi Library in English* (San Francisco: Harper and Row, 1988), 124-38.

6. Although not as much as one might think. See the discussion by Wesley W. Isenberg, "The Gospel of Philip," in Robinson, ed., *Nag Hammadi Library*, 139-60, esp. 139.

finds Philip and tells him to follow him (v. 43). Philip, who is from Bethsaida (v. 44), goes and finds Nathanael, and tells him that they have found the one the prophets promised (vv. 45-46). Jesus demonstrates his prophetic abilities when he meets him (v. 48). In John 6, Jesus asks Philip how they are going to feed the crowd (v. 5), and Philip expresses dismay that they do not have enough money (v. 7). In John 12, some Greeks come to Philip and ask to see Jesus. Philip then goes to Andrew, who tells others. In John 14, Philip asks Jesus to show them the Father so that they will be satisfied (v. 8), to which Jesus replies that one who has seen him has seen the Father. Although there are a number of incidents that thus refer to Philip, he is clearly not a central figure. In virtually every episode he mediates between other parties.

Philip, as a marginalized person, is ripe for rehabilitation. The *Gospel of Philip* concludes with the words "The Gospel according to Philip." The only other reference to a disciple in the entire gospel is to Philip (73.8). This time Philip enjoys a central role in proclaiming the relationship of Joseph to the wood used in the crucifixion. The editor thinks that the book is attributed to Philip simply on the basis that he is the only disciple named. Again, it is noteworthy that it is a figure who plays a minor role in John's Gospel that is used in this Gnostic document.

C. The *Gospel of Mary*

Mary Magdalene is referred to a number of times in the New Testament. She is one of those who witnesses the crucifixion and then goes to Jesus' tomb (Matthew 27:56, 61; 28:1; Mark 15:40, 47; 16:1). In Luke's and John's Gospel she is depicted as reporting what she has seen at Jesus' empty tomb to the other disciples (Luke 24:10; John 19:25; 20:1, 16, 18). Nothing else is said about the relationship between Jesus and Mary.

The fact that Mary was present but not the center of attention must have been too inviting for the Gnostics to pass up.[7] They took the smallest evidence of association between Jesus and Mary and created an en-

---

7. Mary is given a more central role in other Gnostic documents as well, such as the *Gospel of Philip*.

tire story around it. In the *Gospel of Mary*, she is depicted in two ways that focus and expand her role.[8] In the first part of the dialogue she speaks with the risen Jesus. The second part is a description of special revelation given to Mary. Peter begins this section with the acknowledgment to Mary that "the Savior loved you more than the rest of women. Tell us the words of the Savior which you remember — which you know (but) we do not, nor have we heard them" (10.1-6). From simply being the messenger, she is promoted to being the one with special knowledge.

2. Other Marginalized Figures

Several other marginalized figures are given exalted positions in the Gnostic literature. One of these is James. Nothing could be more marginal than not being mentioned at all. James, the brother of Jesus, is not mentioned at all in the canonical Gospels. However, he is mentioned a number of times in the rest of the New Testament. He is seen as the leader of the church at Jerusalem (e.g., Acts 12:17; 15:13; 21:18; 1 Corinthians 15:7; Galatians 1:19; 2:9, 12) and the servant of Christ (James 1:1) and brother of Jude (Jude 1).

In the Gnostic literature James the brother of Jesus is given a number of his own writings. The *Apocryphon of James* is a work of hidden knowledge[9] in which Jesus takes Peter and James apart from the other disciples so that he can give them special knowledge. The book is apparently attributed directly to James as its author. The *First* and *Second Apocalypses of James* are both apocalyptic works.[10] In the first, James and Jesus engage in a dialogue during which James is given special instructions to

8. Karen L. King, George W. MacRae, R. McL. Wilson, and Douglas M. Parrott, "The Gospel of Mary," in Robinson, ed., *Nag Hammadi Library*, 523-27.

9. Francis E. Williams, "The Apocryphon of James," in Robinson, ed., *Nag Hammadi Library*, 29-37.

10. William R. Schoedel and Douglas M. Parrott, "The (First) Apocalypse of James," in Robinson, ed., *Nag Hammadi Library*, 260-68; Charles W. Hedrick and Douglas M. Parrott, "The (Second) Apocalypse of James," in Robinson, ed., *Nag Hammadi Library*, 269-76.

allow him to confront the adversity he is facing. In the second, James is given a set of special revelations from Jesus.

3. The *Gospel of Judas* as Rehabilitation Literature

The *Gospel of Judas* constitutes rehabilitation literature as well. One of the comments often made about this Gnostic document is that it potentially provides unique and new insight into the character of Judas and his relationship to Jesus. It is true that this Gospel depicts Judas in a different light than do the canonical Gospels, for this gospel constitutes an attempt to rehabilitate Judas to a position more central than that in the canonical Gospels. There are several key indicators of this rehabilitation of Judas. Each one indicates that the author of the *Gospel of Judas* knew that Judas was an outsider and needed rehabilitation.

A. Scenes of Betrayal

The first instance is the recognition that Judas is the betrayer of Jesus. There are three important scenes in the *Gospel of Judas* where Judas is acknowledged as the betrayer of Jesus. The first is the scene where, according to the sub-title given by the translators, Judas asks about his fate.[11] Judas comes to Jesus and asks whether he (literally "my seed") is under the control of the rulers of that generation, that is, the earthly realm. By asking the question — reminiscent of the disciples' questions to Jesus at the last supper regarding his betrayal — Judas evidences the skepticism regarding him. Jesus seems to indicate that Judas is in some way under the rulers' control. Jesus tells Judas that he will be cursed by the other generations. There is little doubt that this reveals the response of early readers of the canonical Gospel accounts to the story of Judas. Judas is under the control of this age and has been cursed by the others from that

11. Rodolphe Kasser, Marvin Meyer, and Gregor Wurst, with François Gaudard, "Gospel of Judas," in Kasser, Meyer, and Wurst, eds., *The Gospel of Judas from Codex Tchacos* (Washington: National Geographic, 2006), 32-33.

time to the present. The *Gospel of Judas* attempts to rehabilitate him at this point by saying that he will eventually rule over the thirteen disciples. In other words, Jesus is depicted as telling Judas that, even though he is cursed by the other disciples because of his betrayal of Jesus, in the last days Judas himself will come to rule over them. There is an inversion of place such that the position of the disciples is taken by Judas.

The second scene recognizing Judas as betrayer is even more revelatory. Judas comes to Jesus with what he calls a "great vision," and Jesus instructs him to reveal it to him.[12] Judas tells Jesus that in this vision he saw himself as the twelve disciples stoned him and severely persecuted him. The text at this point has a number of lacunae or holes in the papyrus, so it is not possible to understand the rest of the vision, except that he finds himself in the midst of a crowd and there is a house with greenery on its roof. Jesus tells Judas that no person is able to enter the house since it is reserved for the holy. There are several points to make about this story. One is the acknowledged guilt that Judas has when with the disciples. The scene at the last supper in the canonical Gospels records that all the disciples were present but that Judas had to dismiss himself because he was in the midst of betraying Jesus. Here he has a vision where he admits guilt in the presence of the rest of the disciples, to the point that he sees them as severely persecuting him. His vision goes on to depict an idyllic state that Judas wishes to enter. However, Jesus tells him that he is not worthy of entering this state, which is reserved for those who are holy.

The third betrayal scene clinches the recognition. At the conclusion of the *Gospel of Judas,* in the last scene — entitled "Judas betrays Jesus" by the translators — the priests are waiting for Jesus.[13] They approach Judas and ask what he is doing and recognize him as a disciple of Jesus. Judas acknowledges this, receives money, and hands Jesus over to them. The verb that is used in Coptic is a Greek loan word, the same one that is used in the canonical Gospels to describe Jesus as being handed over or betrayed by Judas. Thus, the *Gospel of Judas* itself ends with the recogni-

12. Kasser, Meyer, and Wurst, with Gaudard, "Gospel of Judas," 31-32.
13. Kasser, Meyer, and Wurst, with Gaudard, "Gospel of Judas," 44-45.

tion that Judas — no matter what motives he may have had — was the betrayer of Jesus.

B. Judas and Special Knowledge

The second major piece of evidence of the attempt at rehabilitation of Judas is the singling out of Judas above the other disciples for having and receiving special knowledge. It is Judas rather than Peter, as in Mark 8 and the parallels, who makes the declaration that he knows who Jesus is.[14] Judas declares that Jesus has come from the "immortal realm of Barbelo" and that he, Judas, is not worthy to mention God's name. For this declaration, Jesus takes Judas aside to tell him the "mysteries of the kingdom." It is Judas who comes to Jesus with his "great vision" that he hears and responds to (as noted already above). Jesus then teaches Judas about cosmology, opening up to him secrets that no one else has seen before. Then Jesus embarks on a lengthy cosmological description that involves Adam (Adamas), the luminaries, the cosmos, chaos, the underworld, the rulers and angels, and creation (to cite the headings of the sections).[15] It is Judas who then asks about how long humanity will live on the earth and about the destruction of the wicked, and Jesus tells him about God's plans.[16] There is no other single disciple, or even group of disciples, in the *Gospel of Judas* that is allowed to ask so many questions of Jesus about God's plans, taken apart for such instruction, and given this amount of information and special knowledge. In several ways, Judas takes over the place of Jesus' closest disciples in the canonical Gospels, Peter, James, and John, and hence he is rehabilitated to the place of an inner circle of one disciple.

C. Judas and Jesus' Crucifixion

The third major piece of evidence of rehabilitation is the special role in his crucifixion that Jesus gives to Judas. Near the end of the *Gospel of Ju-*

14. Kasser, Meyer, and Wurst, with Gaudard, "Gospel of Judas," 21.
15. Kasser, Meyer, and Wurst, with Gaudard, "Gospel of Judas," 31-39.
16. Kasser, Meyer, and Wurst, with Gaudard, "Gospel of Judas," 40-42.

das, Jesus clearly has one more task for Judas, and only Judas, to per-form.[17] In a passage purportedly about baptism, Jesus gives a special task to Judas. He says that Judas will "exceed all of them," with reference apparently to all those who have been baptized. He says that "you will sacrifice the man that clothes me." The dualism between the physical and the spiritual, the bodily and the heavenly, the bad and the good, is typical of Gnostic thought. Jesus here is giving instructions to Judas ex-plicitly to help him in his crucifixion. Here the crucifixion is seen, not as the betrayal of the son of man into the hands of sinners, but as the well thought out and orchestrated act of one who is being rescued and re-leased from the inhibitions and constraints of earthly existence for a no-bler heavenly calling. Judas is called upon to play an important role in this process. Rather than being the cursed betrayer of Jesus, Judas is here seen as the necessary functionary in the grand plan.

4. Conclusion

Gnosticism has a number of rehabilitation documents that attempt to shift peripheral figures to central positions. The nature of the Gnostics as marginalized Christians was perhaps a contributing factor that led them to identify with biblical characters who were marginalized, with the thought that their rehabilitation would in some way presage or en-sure their own rehabilitation. That rehabilitation never came. The *Gospel of Judas* is another in a line of these types of writings, in which Judas is pulled from the periphery into the center so that he can be given special instructions and even a central role to play in the crucifixion of Jesus. The severity of this act is mitigated in the *Gospel of Judas* by its being de-picted as a necessary and welcome shedding of the body as if one were taking off a garment of clothing. However, no matter how the handing over of Jesus is depicted in the *Gospel of Judas,* it is nevertheless a betrayal — as the *Gospel of Judas* in several ways repeatedly recognizes.

17. Kasser, Meyer, and Wurst, with Gaudard, "Gospel of Judas," 42-44.

CHAPTER EIGHT

The *Gospel of Judas* and Its Relationship to the New Testament Canon

Where does the *Gospel of Judas* fit in the timeline of development of the New Testament canon? One of the disputes about the gospel is whether it is simply a third-, fourth-, or even fifth-century Gnostic document (it is probably fourth-century), possibly a copy of a second-century Gnostic document (it may be), or perhaps a document that in fact records authentic material about Judas (it clearly does not). The testable scientific evidence makes clear that the physical document itself dates to somewhere in the third to fifth centuries. If this document is the one that Irenaeus refers to, then it might be a later version of a second-century document. Is there a chance that it could be dated earlier than this? No, that is virtually impossible. The simple and clear reason is that the *Gospel of Judas* is clearly derivative from all of the canonical Gospels. There are some disputes about the dating of the writing of the canonical Gospels, as noted above. However, it is commonly acknowledged that all of the Gospels were written by about A.D. 90. As we show below, the *Gospel of Judas* must have been written sometime after this date, as it uses all of the Gospels in one form or another.[1]

---

1. Most of these references are taken from the commentary on the *Gospel of Judas* in the helpful translation provided by Rodolphe Kasser, Marvin Meyer, and Gregor Wurst, with François Gaudard, "Gospel of Judas," in Kasser, Meyer, and Wurst, eds., *The Gospel of Judas from Codex Tchacos* (Washington: National Geographic, 2006). Others are from our own observations.

1. Thirteen Episodes Reflecting
the Use of the Gospels and Acts

There are at least thirteen episodes in the *Gospel of Judas* worth noting in which it reflects the use of the Gospels.

Episode One. In the introductory episode to scene one, Jesus speaks with his disciples. Then they are gathered together and seated and a thanksgiving prayer is offered over the bread. The Coptic word that is used for "thanksgiving prayer" is a loanword from Greek, and a form of the word that has made its way into English as "eucharist." The verb form of this word appears in the last supper of Jesus at Matthew 15:36; Mark 14:23; Luke 22:17, 19; and 1 Corinthians 11:24. This episode is also reminiscent of the recognition scene between Jesus and two of his disciples as they travel on the Emmaus Road (Luke 24:13-35). As the translators of the *Gospel of Judas* note, "The scene recalls, in part, accounts of the Last Supper, particularly the blessing over the bread, or descriptions of some other holy meal within Judaism and Christianity. The specific language used here calls to mind even more the celebration of the eucharist within Christianity."[2] This observation indicates two important things. One is that the account in the *Gospel of Judas* appears to be derivative from the canonical Gospels. The other is that the language also seems to be later than the time of the New Testament, once institutions such as communion had been more formalized.

Episode Two. Later in the same scene, the disciples offer a confession of who Jesus is: "Master you are [. . .] the son of our god." This kind of overt declaration of the identity of Jesus is certainly to be found in the New Testament. As the editors note, it is Peter who makes this affirmation in Matthew 16:13-20; Mark 8:27-30; and Luke 9:18-21.[3] There are several observations to make about the confession in the *Gospel of Judas*. One is that the confession is made by all the disciples, not by a single individual as in the canonical Gospels. The second is that the confession is that Jesus is the "son of our god," that is, the god of this generation. The

2. Kasser, Meyer, and Wurst, with Gaudard, "Gospel of Judas," 21 n. 10.
3. Kasser, Meyer, and Wurst, with Gaudard, "Gospel of Judas," 21 n. 14.

confession of Peter is that Jesus is the Christ, the son of the living God (as Matthew 16:16 expands it). A third observation is that the *Gospel of Judas* appears to follow the confession as given in Matthew's Gospel, rather than the shorter confession in Mark's Gospel (or similarly in Luke).

Episode Three. Jesus gives Judas secret knowledge that he will be separated from the other disciples and initiated into the mysteries of the kingdom. He tells Judas that "someone else will replace you, in order that the twelve [disciples] may again come to completion with their god." This is clearly a reference to Acts 1:15-26[4] and the choice by the casting of lots of Matthias to be Judas's replacement in the group of twelve disciples.

Episode Four. In the introduction to scene two, Jesus comes to his disciples, who tell him that they have seen him in a vision. In a severely damaged section that has been restored by the editors, Jesus asks them "Why have [you . . . when] <you> have gone into hiding?"[5] The editors suggest that, if their restoration is correct, there may be a reference here to how the disciples ran away with fright when Jesus was arrested. They refer to Matthew 26:56 and Mark 14:50-52. The actual verse of relevance is Mark 14:50 (not the incident of the young man fleeing naked) and Matthew 26:56. It is difficult to determine which Gospel is being followed, although the author of the *Gospel of Judas* may well have known both of them.

Episode Five. In the section about the disciples seeing the temple, there is a description of this "great house with a large altar in it," priests, "a crowd of people," and the receiving of offerings. There are several scenes in the Gospels where Jesus goes to the Jerusalem temple with his disciples. These passages include Matthew 21:12-17; 24:1–25:46; Mark 11:15-19; 13:1-37; Luke 19:45-48; 21:5-38; and John 2:13-22.[6] The editors note that Jesus speaks of "what the disciples 'have seen.'" It is not likely that the reference here is to Jesus' cleansing of the temple, but it is more likely a paraphrase of Jesus' apocalyptic discourse in Mark 13, Matthew 24, and Luke 21. The opening of Mark's apocalyptic discourse with Jesus' reference to the "great buildings" (13:2) seems to lie behind the *Gospel of Judas*.

---

4. Kasser, Meyer, and Wurst, with Gaudard, "Gospel of Judas," 23 n. 25.
5. Kasser, Meyer, and Wurst, with Gaudard, "Gospel of Judas," 25 n. 35.
6. Kasser, Meyer, and Wurst, with Gaudard, "Gospel of Judas," 25 n. 36.

Episode Six. Jesus interprets the vision of the temple by means of an allegorical method typical of Gnostic interpretation. In his condemnation of the priests at the altar, he notes that they "have planted trees without fruit. . . ." This alludes to the passage in Matthew 21:19 and the fig tree. Jesus sees the fig tree by the road but finds no figs. He states that "No longer shall there ever be any fruit from you."

Episode Seven. In the closing action of scene two, Jesus says to Judas that "it is impossible to sow seed on [rock] and harvest its fruit." This language, as the editors note, is reminiscent of the parable of the sower found in Matthew 13:3-23; Mark 4:1-20; and Luke 8:4-15.[7] The reference is so short that it is impossible to tell which of the Gospels lies behind it.

Episode Eight. In discussing his own fate with Jesus, Jesus tells Judas that "In the last days they will curse your ascent to the holy [generation]." The editors admit that their translation is not certain, but they think that it alludes to either a transformation or an ascent.[8] The language seems to be stronger than simply an allusion, but a forced attempt to depict Judas as involved in some kind of spiritual transformation. If it is an ascent, it may be based upon 2 Corinthians 12:2-4, as the editors suggest, or simply upon the ascension of Jesus himself. If it is a transformation, it may be based upon Jesus' transfiguration (see Judas's transfiguration, below).

Episode Nine. Jesus' cosmology in the *Gospel of Judas* speaks of a "luminous cloud" appearing. The editors note that this may be rendered with "cloud of light" as well. The editors interpret the cloud as some kind of a manifestation of the divine. More likely is that the author of the *Gospel of Judas* is simply imbuing his account with what he has found in Matthew 17:5-6; Mark 9:7-8; Luke 9:34-35 — a cloud that accompanies Jesus' transfiguration.[9]

Episode Ten. Judas is depicted as having his very own transfiguration. He lifts up his eyes and sees the "luminous cloud" and enters it. Then there is a voice from the cloud that says something about him (the text is

---

7. Kasser, Meyer, and Wurst, with Gaudard, "Gospel of Judas," 30 n. 69.

8. Kasser, Meyer, and Wurst, with Gaudard, "Gospel of Judas," 33 n. 85.

9. Kasser, Meyer, and Wurst, with Gaudard, "Gospel of Judas," 34 n. 89.

damaged at this point). The transformation in the canonical Gospels (see Matthew 17:1-8; Mark 9:2-8; Luke 9:28-36) involves Jesus taking Peter, James, and John to a mountain where Jesus is transfigured before them. There is a cloud, and from the cloud a voice states that "This is my beloved Son, listen to him" (Mark 9:7). In the *Gospel of Judas,* we see that Judas has displaced not just the other disciples, but Jesus himself as the object of transfiguration, and that the words from the cloud probably said something about him.[10]

Episode Eleven. In the concluding episode, the high priests are depicted as grumbling because Jesus has gone into the "guest room" for prayer. The word that is used here for "guest room" is a loanword from Greek of the same word that is used in Mark 14:14 and Luke 22:11 for the room where the last supper was held.[11]

Episode Twelve. The *Gospel of Judas* says that the scribes were careful in arresting Jesus, "for they were afraid of the people, since he was regarded by all as a prophet." As the editors point out, this seems to reflect language found in Matthew 26:1-5; Mark 14:1-2; Luke 22:1-2; and John 11:45-53[12] — more likely the Synoptic Gospels than John at this point.

Episode Thirteen. The closing words of the *Gospel of Judas* speak of Judas receiving money from the high priests and betraying Jesus to them. The editors state that the "conclusion of the *Gospel of Judas* is presented in subtle and understated terms, and there is no account of the actual crucifixion of Jesus."[13] It is true that there is no crucifixion depicted, but this is a book that concentrates on Judas — and it ends with the nadir of his career, an account of his handing over of Jesus for money. Any attempt to mitigate Judas's involvement, even in this gospel, must reckon with the fact that Judas is depicted not only as doing what Jesus asks him to do in helping him to rid himself of his human clothing, but as receiving payment from the high priests for doing so. This act, even in the *Gospel of Judas,* compromises the motives of Judas in participating in the betrayal of Jesus.

---

10. See Kasser, Meyer, and Wurst, with Gaudard, "Gospel of Judas," 44 n. 145 on the possible content of the words.

11. Kasser, Meyer, and Wurst, with Gaudard, "Gospel of Judas," 44 n. 147.

12. Kasser, Meyer, and Wurst, with Gaudard, "Gospel of Judas," 44 n. 149.

13. Kasser, Meyer, and Wurst, with Gaudard, "Gospel of Judas," 45 n. 150.

2. Conclusion

The evidence indicates that the *Gospel of Judas* is almost entirely derivative from the canonical Gospels and Acts, along with plenty of Gnostic theologizing. In a few instances it is possible to tell which of the canonical Gospels that the author of the *Gospel of Judas* used in creating his account of Judas. In many instances, however, it is impossible to tell what account he is relying upon, because his references are so broad. The references are there, nevertheless. In that sense, the *Gospel of Judas* reflects a common pattern in which the later apocryphal gospels, such as the *Egerton Gospel* from the second century, draw upon and even allude to or cite the canonical Gospels.

CHAPTER NINE

Orthodoxy versus Heresy: Lost Christianities and the "Lucky Winner" Thesis

One of the most disconcerting questions for many in the discussion of Gnosticism and the *Gospel of Judas* is "which version of Christianity is authentic?" Which form of Christianity, if any, is the one that Jesus sought to initiate by his arrival, ministry, death, and resurrection? Can orthodox or traditional Christians legitimately claim that theirs is the true version and that all other forms are heretical? Or can one read the Gnostic works and see in them an alternative, but no less true, form of Christianity? In fact, is perhaps the Gnostic form closer to the type that Jesus sought to create? The question is not whether Jesus existed (although some contemporary sympathizers with Gnosticism would go so far as to say that Jesus never even existed), but rather whose expression of Christianity is to be taken as most "true."

The twentieth-century findings of Gnostic writings have made these types of questions all the more pressing. With the discovery of so many different Gnostic and otherwise variations of documents that seemed to identify with Christianity in some way, how does one say a particular document is more "true" than another? The recent discovery of the *Gospel of Judas* only exacerbates the issue; for why do we not take its version of Judas's actions during the last days of Jesus' life as the "true" version of what transpired? Perhaps we have been wrong all these years.

For centuries, the answer to this line of questioning would have been that orthodoxy had won because it was right and that the only form of authentic Christianity was the type based on the teachings of the twenty-seven books of the New Testament. For centuries, the consensus in both eastern and western versions of Christianity was that the church had faced serious struggles with heresy (including the Gnostic threat) in its earliest centuries but had managed to preserve the apostles' message. There was a basic assumption that defenders of orthodoxy like Irenaeus, Tertullian, Epiphanius, Athanasius, and others had been right in their fight and had blessed the church by their unrelenting efforts to preserve the apostles' message as it had been transmitted.

Over the course of the nineteenth and twentieth centuries, however, there have been an increasing number of scholars who do not think Irenaeus and others were a blessing to the church. For some, they were no longer identified as "defenders of the faith" but rather pejoratively called "heresy-hunters." Their motives in criticizing the heretics have even been called into question, as has their claim to being holders of the "truth." In the recent discourse surrounding the *Gospel of Judas*, there have been those who stated these very things: the *Gospel of Judas* was suppressed by the "heresy hunters" of the early church.

The following sections will address these questions. The first section will outline in detail the convictions of one representative scholar who sees these recent discoveries of Gnostic (and other) texts as the recovery of lost Christian voices that have an equal claim to being as "Christian" as the orthodox claim. The second section will critique that position and defend a more traditional and orthodox understanding of these texts and what they mean for the identity of "true" Christianity.

1. Lost Christianities?

One scholar who has had a considerable amount of influence on the discourse surrounding the *Gospel of Judas* is Bart D. Ehrman, professor of religious studies at the University of North Carolina. Besides writing a chapter in National Geographic's newly released book entitled *The Gos-*

pel of Judas, he wrote the Foreword to *The Lost Gospel,* the other book published by the Society to tell the story of the new find.[1] His comments have also been sought after by numerous media sources, and quotations by Ehrman permeate a significant number of newspaper articles. Very early in the process of restoring the *Gospel of Judas,* he was invited by the National Geographic Society to bring his expertise in early Christian history to the team of scholars who were translating the document.

No doubt Ehrman was sought after due to his knowledge of Gnostic and early Christian literature. The problems for holders of a traditional view of orthodoxy are that Ehrman's commentary is decidedly nontraditional, and that his nontraditional opinion is one of the major shapers of public opinion regarding the new find. As a result of Ehrman's significance, it is important to spend a few moments on how he understands the battle between orthodoxy and heresy in the early centuries of the church's existence.

The best way to understand Ehrman's perspective is to review his book on the matter entitled *Lost Christianities: The Battles for Scripture and the Faiths We Never Knew.* In *Lost Christianities,* he examines the variety of non-canonical writings and explores how "one early Christian group established itself as dominant in the religion."[2] The basic premise of the book is that the orthodox church was able, through a variety of factors, to gain the upper hand in its battles with what they deemed heretical movements and in turn to become the only "true" church. This argument can be called the "lucky winner" thesis. Ehrman points out what was "gained" by this victory — things such as a shared creed, Nicene theology, a canon of Scripture, and a uniform liturgy. He also points out the "losses" that occurred as a result of this victory by the orthodox, includ-

1. Ehrman, "Christianity Turned on Its Head: The Alternative Vision of the Gospel of Judas," in Rodolphe Kasser, Marvin Meyer, and Gregor Wurst, eds., *The Gospel of Judas from Codex Tchacos* (Washington: National Geographic, 2006), 77-120, and "Foreword," in Herbert Krosney, *The Lost Gospel: The Quest for the Gospel of Judas Iscariot* (Washington: National Geographic, 2006), xv-xxiii.

2. Bart D. Ehrman, *Lost Christianities: The Battles for Scripture and the Faiths We Never Knew* (New York: Oxford University Press, 2003), ix.

ing the loss of diversity and destruction or disappearance of various "heretical" texts. Ehrman also notes how the orthodox victory shaped the following 1600 years of church history and, in many ways, the course of western civilization. He writes:

> If some other form of Christianity had won the early struggles for dominance, the familiar doctrines of Christianity might never have become the "standard" belief of millions of people, including the belief that there is only one God, that he is the creator, that Christ his son is both human and divine. . . . The creeds still spoken in churches today might never have been devised. The New Testament as a collection of sacred books might never have come into being. Or it might have come into being with an entirely different set of books. . . . Had the conflicts been resolved differently, as odd as this may seem, people in the West — we ourselves — might have remained polytheists to this day, worshiping the ancient gods of Greece and Rome. On the other hand, the empire might have converted to a different form of Christianity and the development of Western society and culture might have developed in ways that we cannot imagine.[3]

However, Ehrman is no dispassionate observer, for while he makes it quite clear that things would have been different if the orthodox had not "won," he also argues that the type of Christianity exhibited by the orthodox Christians was very intolerant. He is elated at the new discoveries of documents being made, and it is his hope that they will contribute to a growing appreciation for disparate voices then, and now.

While Ehrman's openness to new forms of Christianity may resonate with some, there are significant assumptions and conclusions in his *Lost Christianities* that are problematic for those committed to a more traditional understanding of Christianity. These assumptions and conclusions will be dealt with in the following section.

---

3. Ehrman, *Lost Christianities*, 6.

2. A Critique of the "Lucky Winner" Thesis

A. What We Are Not Saying

Anyone familiar with the dynamics of debating realizes that often it is just as important (and sometimes more) to state what you are *not* saying than what you are saying. This may be one of those times. Despite what follows, we are not saying that there is no merit to Ehrman's work. On the contrary, a particular strength of *Lost Christianities* is that it provides the reader with a sense of the many diverse elements that identified with Christianity in some way. There were many different writings and movements in the early church, and Ehrman's discussion of works such as *Acts of Paul* or the *Secret Gospel of Mark*[4] and of the Marcionites and the Gnostics reminds one of the very real divisions and problems the church faced.

Second, we are not saying that the early church fathers did everything right or were correct in every doctrine that they taught. For instance, Irenaeus believed that Jesus lived to be quite a bit older than is traditionally thought.

Third, we are not saying that the early fathers agreed on everything. There was disagreement over doctrine and practice. In fact, the New Testament book of Acts and the letters of Paul provide ample evidence that there was disagreement in the very first years of the church's existence.

Fourth, we are not saying that all Gnostics were evil and sought to destroy the church. There is no reason to doubt that many who sought to Gnosticize Christianity were genuine and sincere in their convictions that they really had some special truth or knowledge that would lead to liberation.

Fifth, we are not saying that the recent finds of Gnostic writings, including the *Gospel of Judas,* are not fantastic discoveries. They are incredibly helpful finds that provide a great deal of information about the types and extent of Gnostic writings.

---

4. Ehrman (*Lost Christianities,* 67-89) raises questions about its authenticity. See our Chapter Six.

B. What Is at Stake

What is at stake are the very claims of the Christian faith as it has generally been known for close to 2000 years. If Ehrman is correct in his claim that orthodox Christianity is just the "lucky winner" of the theological battles and has no real claim to being any more "true" than any other version of Christianity, then the creeds, liturgies, hymns, and even Scripture used in churches should have a disclaimer printed next to them that reads "all claims to truth in this text are from the perspective of the author — if your perspective differs that is okay and is true for you." In other words, the Gnostics, with their belief in one, two, or more gods, can have an equal claim to being the "true" version of the faith or their belief that Jesus was not really human can have an equally legitimate claim to being the "true" faith. For someone committed to some type of postmodern relativism this is not necessarily a problem. However, it is problematic for anyone who holds to an orthodox view of the Christian faith.

C. What We Are Saying about the "Lucky Winner" Thesis

What are we saying about the "lucky winner" thesis? What we will argue in the remainder of this chapter is that the orthodox church was more than just the "lucky winner" of those early theological battles. It was also more than just one option among other equally valid options in regards to the type of Christianity available (then and today). It is our firm conviction that, even with all of its sins, faults, and divisions, the orthodox church that emerged victorious was the church that best held to the teaching of the apostles in regards to what Christ lived and said.

On what basis can one say such a thing? Certainly there have been theological arguments made in support of this assertion. The Christian doctrine of providence has often been referred to when discussions of the canon have been raised. The argument from providence is that God oversaw the formation of the canon and allowed only the books that he wanted to be included so that the church would have a standard of apostolic teaching. Providence has also been used to support the contention that the orthodox church is more than just the lucky winner of the theological battles:

it was God-ordained that the faithful and orthodox would win against the heretics. The difficulty with the "providence argument" is that it is difficult to support from evidence. How does one really know that that is what God was up to, and what evidence does one point to for support (other than to point to what happened)? Without denying that God providentially works in the life of the world and in his church, the contention being made here is that the winner of the theological battles in the early church was the church that best held to the teaching of the apostles in regard to what Jesus Christ has lived and said can also be supported from the historical evidence.

Since the following discussion will focus on historical evidence, a few comments on the nature of historical research are in order. While one can expect a degree of certainty in disciplines such as chemistry or physics, the degree of certainty in history is markedly different. When seeking to reconstruct the past, a historian has only evidence to interpret. As in a court of law, this evidence is open to interpretation, and evidence can lead only to conclusions based on probability, not absolute certainty. In other words, there is no way to "prove" the above claim regarding the orthodox church (if by "prove" one means to come to a conclusion that is as objective as a conclusion in chemistry or physics), and there will not be incontrovertible evidence found (especially events in ancient history).[5] Rather, one must determine whether something happened by weighing evidence and coming to a conclusion as to what was most probable. To expect anything more is unfair and unscholarly.

One problem with evidence, however, is that it must be weighed, for evidence does not interpret itself. Here is where the problem of bias enters into the discussion. No historian is without biases, and every historian brings interpretative biases to the weighing of evidence (e.g., What goes first? What is important? Whose work is authoritative? How

5. We are not proposing that we need to accept the postmodernist claim that we cannot know anything with confidence about the past. We are saying that evidence is essential to any claim and that there is rarely enough evidence to answer every question about the past. For a very helpful book on the need for evidence and the possibility and limits of historical knowledge, see Richard Evans, *In Defence of History* (London: Granta, 1997). For a helpful discussion from an overtly Christian perspective, see David Bebbington, *Patterns in History: A Christian Perspective on Historical Thought* (Leicester: Apollos, 1990).

should this sentence be translated?). One problem with current scholarship surrounding the recent discoveries of Gnostic writings (and Ehrman's work seems to be no exception) is that there is a significant amount of bias influencing decisions, and in most cases the bias is not acknowledged. Jenkins has noted how many who are the most fervent critics of traditional Christianity have considerable baggage that would impact the way in which they weigh evidence:

> In understanding such dedicated attacks on traditional Christianity, it is difficult to avoid observing that the scholars in question are often struggling (and perhaps overreacting) against their own fundamentalist backgrounds, and thus have a natural sympathy for the most liberal perspectives. Among the more radical New Testament critics, we often find similar stories: [Burton] Mack was a minister in the conservative Church of the Nazarene; [Bishop John Shelby] Spong often writes about his strictly fundamentalist upbringing in the North Carolina of the 1940s and 1950s; [James M.] Robinson's own background was conservative and evangelical; [John Dominic] Crossan is a former Catholic priest. [Robert W.] Funk himself had been not only a fundamentalist, but a preacher who led revivals in rural Texas. These personal histories may explain the group's natural preference for a religious style based on seeking, rather than on dogmatic authority, and their rejection of a narrowly defined canon of inspired scriptures. This interpretation adds a pointed irony to the Jesus Seminar's warning to scholars, "Beware of finding a Jesus entirely congenial to you," since that is conspicuously what Funk, Mack, Crossan, and the others have been doing.[6]

What makes one think that Ehrman's own bias may be a factor in his favoring of a more liberal understanding is his own rejection of his fundamentalist background[7] and his desire to have a more tolerant Christianity.

In his closing chapter, Ehrman laments the intolerance of what he

---

6. Philip Jenkins, *Hidden Gospels: How the Search for Jesus Lost Its Way* (New York: Oxford University Press, 2001), 168.

7. G. Jeffrey MacDonald, "Christian Mavericks Find Affirmation in Ancient Heresies," *Christian Science Monitor* (April 14, 2006). Retrieved from csmonitor.com.

calls the "proto-orthodox" church. He also states that their religious intolerance toward pagans and heretics might seem "intolerable to us today."[8] His hope is that the church would move beyond such intolerance and be open to more diversity of expressions. He writes:

> This fascination is not simply a matter of antiquarian interest. There is instead a sense that alternative understandings of Christianity from the past can be cherished yet today, that they can provide insights even now for those of us who are concerned about the world and our place in it. Those captivated with this fascination commonly feel a sense of loss upon realizing just how many perspectives once endorsed by well-meaning, intelligent, and sincere believers came to be abandoned, destroyed, and forgotten — as were the texts that these believers produced, read, and revered. But with that feeling of loss comes the joy of discovery when some of these texts, and the lost Christianities they embody, are recovered and restored to us. For our own religious histories encompass not only the forms of belief and practice that emerged as victorious from the conflicts of the past but also those that were overcome, suppressed, and eventually lost.[9]

What it seems Ehrman is saying is that to hold to the traditional paradigm of the orthodox church as the holder of the apostolic tradition and the various Gnostic and other movements as heretical is to be very out-of-touch with contemporary notions of tolerance and is detrimental to the spiritual journey of those who look to them for inspiration. In other words, to conclude anything other than what he concludes about the "lost Christianities" is completely unacceptable due to the consequences. The problem with such a view is that it has nothing to do with scholarly historical research. To misunderstand the distinction between historical research and the consequences (or hopes) of one's research is to make one susceptible to the very common error of interpreting the past with the aim of confirming one's present-day convictions. Of course, one's bi-

---

8. Ehrman, *Lost Christianities*, 256.
9. Ehrman, *Lost Christianities*, 256.

ases always affect a study of the past and a sifting of the evidence. However, good scholars do everything possible to minimize this and to account for it; it is questionable whether Ehrman has done either.

Underlying the question as to whether there can be one "true" version of Christianity is the assumption or bias that there *can* be one version that is more authentic than another. For a variety of reasons, Ehrman and others are committed to a position that denies the possibility of there being an orthodox or authentic version of the Christian faith. However, the way in which "authentic" is being used here is that it refers to the version of Christianity that most closely (but not necessarily perfectly) held to the teaching of Jesus. In the most basic sense, Christianity is a religion based on following the teachings of Jesus. The most "authentic" form of Christianity, therefore, is the one that most closely holds to the teaching of Jesus. In regard to the orthodoxy versus heresy debate or the "lucky winner" thesis, what the historian has to do is demonstrate which Christian community had the best claim of following the teachings of Jesus. If it can be demonstrated that one community had a better claim, then it is most probable that that community was the orthodox group (one that held to the "right" teaching of Jesus) and the others were legitimately called heretical.

To a large degree the issue is one of documents. What Christian documents is it most reasonable and fair to see as foundational and authoritative? Which documents have the best claim to speak for "true" Christianity? Remember, the claim of Ehrman and others is that the second- and third-century Gnostic documents were equally valid and authentic expressions of the Christian faith and that no one set of documents was more orthodox or authentic than another. But was that really the case? The evidence would indicate that it was not.

In order to determine which documents were the most genuine expressions of the Christian faith, one has to ask some specific questions regarding the actual documents. The key questions regarding authenticity and documents revolve around issues such as dating, authorship, and reliability.

i. Dating One of the most compelling arguments for rejecting the "lucky winner" thesis is that the twenty-seven documents that eventually comprised the New Testament were all written in the first century. On the other hand, the *Gospel of Judas* and the additional various Gnostic (and other) writings were from the second and third centuries or later. In other words, the Gnostic writings were written three, four, five, six, or more generations after the New Testament documents were written. The point here is simple: how could documents written generations after Jesus' life be considered as authoritative as those written a few decades after Jesus' life?

ii. Authorship The twenty-seven documents that would become the New Testament were also deemed authoritative in the early church because they were understood to have been written by those closest to the life of Jesus. As far as anyone knows, Jesus never recorded his teachings or wrote an autobiography. The next best thing for his followers, therefore, was to get a summary of Jesus' teaching from those closest to him. These earliest writings were considered to have been written by those who were eyewitnesses of Jesus' life, by those who could research the events not too long after Jesus' death, or, in the case of the Apostle Paul, by someone who had experienced Jesus in a miraculous first-hand way. The term the early church used to express this intimacy with Jesus and an accurate transmission of his teaching was "apostolicity." A work that was apostolic, or fit the criterion of apostolicity, was a definitive work — the standard or the canon by which all other works needed to be judged. In an ironic way, even the apocryphal and pseudonymous "heretics" who used the names of apostles and intimates of Jesus confirmed this, for they were the ones who tried to legitimize their works by making it sound as if they fit the criterion of apostolicity.

The question is simply this: who gets to define the nature of Christianity? This is not the same as asking whether the apostles were right in what they wrote; it is simply asking who got the "right" to define the new religion. Ehrman and others who grant the New Testament documents and the multitude of other Gnostic writings the same level of authority make a fundamental error when they answer this question. It seems commonsense (and fair) to allow for the earliest founders of a religion to define the parameters of belief and practice for a new religion. This is even more the case for the earliest Christians, who made theological and historical claims based on what they had actually seen and experienced in the life of Jesus (in many cases they were eyewitness accounts). On what basis should these people be denied the privilege and right as founders to determine the essence of the new faith?

iii. Reliability   Even early documents written by eyewitnesses could be unreliable and untrustworthy. However, there is good reason to believe that the documents that eventually became the New Testament are historically reliable.[10] This is not the same as arguing that the texts were perfect and without error. All that is being argued here is that, as historical documents (the technical term in historical research is "primary sources"), the New Testament writings were reliable witnesses to the events that they describe.

For these three reasons — dating, authorship, and reliability — the twenty-seven books of the New Testament eventually became the canon — the standard of apostolic teaching. In other words, if you wanted to know what Jesus did or taught, if you wanted to know what the apostles did or taught, or if you wanted to know where to get a correct understanding of Christian belief, you went to the New Testament canon. Conversely, if you wanted to know what was outside of the boundaries of correct thinking about the faith you had a standard for judging other claims.

The difficulty, however, is that Ehrman rejects claims that give the traditional canon any authority above other texts. In his book on the *Gospel of Judas*, Robinson makes it clear that he, too, distances himself from what he calls the "standard conservative prejudice in favor of limiting oneself to the canonical Gospels to the exclusion of the noncanonical

10. For example, see Craig Blomberg, *The Historical Reliability of the Gospels* (Downers Grove: InterVarsity, 1987); F. F. Bruce, *The New Testament Documents: Are They Reliable?* (Downers Grove: InterVarsity, 1972); Michael J. Wilkins and J. P. Moreland, eds., *Jesus under Fire: Modern Scholarship Reinvents the Historical Jesus* (Grand Rapids: Zondervan, 1995); N. T. Wright, *The Resurrection of the Son of God* (Minneapolis: Fortress, 2004); Colin Brown, *Miracles and the Critical Mind* (Grand Rapids: Eerdmans, 1984).

Gospels."[11] In fact, the panel of experts brought in to work on the *Gospel of Judas* all seem to share this anti-canonical bias.

Questions regarding authorship and reliability are a part of the issue for those who reject the authority of the traditional canon. Many of these questions arise out of a wholehearted acceptance of the results of modern New Testament criticism. However, there is no need to deal with the labyrinth of scholarship around these issues, for it could be argued that authorship and reliability issues (by comparison) are not as important as dating. In fact, one key "bottom line" issue for whose version of Christianity is the most authentic is that of dating. Even if the authors were not all eyewitnesses of the events, and even if the Gospel accounts differ in some matters, the fact that the Gospels were among the first Christian documents gives them the right to define what Christianity is all about (and remember, next to no-one dates the twenty-seven books outside the first century, and almost everyone — including Ehrman — dates the Gnostic writings from the second and third centuries or later). On the basis of a strict chronology (and in an argument addressing authenticity this is of utmost importance), all other later documents can fairly be considered variations from the original documents. Of course, there are good reasons to believe that, along with early dating, the twenty-seven books were also written by apostles and the like and were reliable. There is also good reason to believe that the early church cared about such issues and was competent to address such issues.

A few more brief comments on the process of canonization are in order.[12] Ehrman and others who view the *Gospel of Judas* and other Gnostic writings "at par" with the canonical writings fail to give adequate weight to the following realities in the formation of the New Testament. First, despite the fact that there were many second- and third-century gospels, none that we know of ever circulated together with the four canonical Gospels Matthew, Mark, Luke, and John. Regardless of who wrote the four canonical Gospels, no other gospels ever came close to being recognized

11. James M. Robinson, *The Secrets of Judas: The Story of the Misunderstood Disciple and His Lost Gospel* (San Francisco: HarperCollins, 2006), 73.

12. See also Chapter Three.

as "at par" with the four — even the much vaunted *Gospel of Thomas* was a second-century no-name gospel compared to Matthew, Mark, Luke, and John.[13] It should also be noted that these four Gospels circulated together as a foursome perhaps as early as the end of the first century but most likely by the middle of the second century (and no other gospel ever joined these four). Second, despite the variety of extracanonical works in the second century, Paul's letters circulated together as a Pauline *corpus* (body) by the end of the first century. A fair survey of the process of canonization will show that there were some works not immediately recognized as canonical (such as Revelation and Hebrews) that would eventually make it into the canon and some works that were in some canons (such as the *Shepherd of Hermas* and *First Clement*) that would eventually not make it into the final canon. However, a fair survey of the same process will also show how what was unchanged throughout the centuries was the acceptance of the four Gospels and Paul's works. No Gnostic work ever belonged to this select group of unquestioned and authoritative writings. In short, the Gnostic writings that Ehrman and others esteem so highly were never a part of the earliest informal canon, and no Gnostic writing was ever universally considered for inclusion into the canon.

iv. Other Issues   While much of the issue surrounding the "lucky winner" thesis is a matter of documents, other related factors must be taken into account. The first is that the earliest church saw itself as a continuation of the people of Israel and used the Old Testament as its Bible. One example from Irenaeus illustrates this continuity with Old Testament revelation:

---

13. The recent Jesus Seminar publication of the *Gospel of Thomas* with the four canonical Gospels (Robert W. Funk, Roy W. Hoover, and The Jesus Seminar, *The Five Gospels* [New York: Macmillan, 1993]) is based on hopeful thinking, sensationalized scholarship, and (perhaps) commercial goals, rather than on any historical reasons. The earliest Christians never included the *Gospel of Thomas* in their canon, and based on all evidence they never would have included it. To argue that they "should have" but did not know any better is condescending and judgmental and goes against positive evidence that indicates that the early church was quite competent and capable of deciding issues of authorship and apostolic authority.

But since the writings of Moses are the words of Christ, He does Himself declare to the Jews, as John has recorded in the Gospel: "If ye had believed Moses, ye would have believed Me: for he wrote of Me. But if ye believe not his writings, neither will ye believe My words." He thus indicates in the clearest manner that the writings of Moses are His words. If, then, [this be the case with regard] to Moses, so also, beyond a doubt, the words of the other prophets are His [words], as I have pointed out. And again, the Lord Himself exhibits Abraham as having said to the rich man, with reference to all those who were still alive: "If they do not obey Moses and the prophets, neither, if any one were to rise from the dead and go to them, will they believe him."[14]

The Gnostic rejection of the Old Testament God and the goodness of creation, as well as, in the case of the Cainites, the esteeming of the sinners of the Old Testament, simply could not be reconciled with such a view of the Old Testament. Clearly the Gnostic rejection of the Bible of the earliest church (the Old Testament) and the Jewish roots of the church makes it clear that the Gnostic version was a radically different and later form of the Christian faith.

The second factor is that of the Apostles' Creed and the *Didache*. A creed (from the Latin "credo" meaning "I believe") is a brief summary of core convictions. The Apostles' Creed (ca. A.D. 100),[15] one of the earliest creeds of the church, was an attempt to summarize the apostles' teaching. There is no way that one could confuse the tenets of the Apostles' Creed with the content of the Gnostic writings. In fact, the Apostles' Creed quite clearly reflects the central message of the twenty-seven books that would eventually become the New Testament and was for-

14. Irenaeus, *Against Heresies* 4.2.3.

15. While the creed in its present form can only be traced to around the beginning of the sixth century, the core elements go back to the apostolic age. See Philip Schaff, ed., *The Creeds of Christendom: With a History and Critical Notes* (New York: Harper and Row, 1931; reprint, Grand Rapids: Baker, 1998), 1:19-20. The fact that the twelve apostles almost certainly did not write this creed does not undermine the point being made here. The Apostles' Creed (regardless of author[s]) simply illustrates how the earliest Christians summarized the essentials of the apostles' message.

mulated long before the struggles with Gnosticism began. The contents of this very early creed, therefore, bolster the claim that the first-century form of Christianity was normative, and the second- and third-century Gnostic versions were radical departures from the norm. The *Didache* was an orthodox document that was most likely written before A.D. 125. This document is clear that there was true and false teaching in the church, which means that there was a basic sense of what was orthodox and what was not. (Other very early documents such as Ignatius's letters reveal the same conviction.) This is not to say that the first-century church was a tranquil homogeneous church with no problems. Ehrman is right in noting that there was diversity in the early church. Nevertheless, the main creed that has come out of the first century reflects the teaching of the apostles as found in the twenty-seven books of the New Testament. What this suggests is that, despite the diversity, there were some basic beliefs that many agreed upon, and that the documents that would become the New Testament were deemed to be normative for the formation of the essentials of the faith.

A third consideration is that Gnostic documents like the *Gospel of Judas* contained a radically different type of Christianity than the type expressed in the first-century documents. The Gnostic documents are also of a different style. If there was no real difference between the first-century twenty-seven books that eventually became the New Testament and the second-century Gnostic writings, it may have been harder to argue that one group was authentic and the other was not. The fact of the matter is that, in terms of content and writing style, they are worlds apart. Even those who reject the authority of the canonical writings note the significant differences.

A fourth consideration concerns the orthodox idea of apostolic succession and tradition. One way in which Gnostics sought to usurp the authority of the apostolic writings was to claim that they, not the orthodox, had the secret message or tradition of Jesus Christ passed on through successive generations of Gnostic leaders. To counter this claim, the early church stressed the idea of apostolic succession. In the earliest churches, the idea was simply that the apostolic tradition had been transmitted by the first apostles to the first bishop of a church and then through an unbroken line of faithful bishops in subsequent years. Thus, a church could point back to its founding through a line of bishops, and throughout these early years it was important for churches to keep a record of successive bishops in order to show its apostolic roots and faithfulness to the tradition of the apostles. These unbroken lines back to a church's origins are another argument against the claim that the new and novel Gnostic version of the faith in the second and third century was an equally valid form of Christianity.

3. Conclusion

Gnosticism has no claim to the earliest Christian texts, creeds, documents, or tradition, nor was Gnosticism remotely close to affirming any core convictions of the orthodox church. Rather than accept "at par" Gnostic writings like the *Gospel of Judas* with the New Testament canon, it seems only fair to say that the earliest documents written by the apostles (or those close to them) should take precedence over every other subsequent document. In other words, the criterion for defining Christianity in the second century was not simply the privilege of whoever won the battles (the "lucky winner" thesis), but whose view of the Christian faith was based on the teaching of the earliest and apostolic writings. For the most part, the Gnostic writings were of a radically different nature and contained radically different messages from the four Gospels and the letters of Paul. On the other hand, in view of its reliance on the authority of those early and apostolic writings, the orthodox church that based its convictions on the teachings of the apostles had a legitimate claim to being the holders of the "true" teaching of the apostles. This point is supported by J. Gresham Machen, an opponent of liberalism in the early part of the twentieth century. In his classic work against liberal theology, *Christianity and Liberalism,* he wrote:

> [i]t is perfectly conceivable that the originators of the Christian movement had no right to legislate for subsequent generations; but at any rate they did have an inalienable right to legislate for all generations

that should choose to bear the name of "Christian." It is conceivable that Christianity may now have to be abandoned, and another religion substituted for it; but at any rate the question of what Christianity is can be determined only by an examination of the beginnings of Christianity.[16]

That being the case, the orthodox rejection of anything that differed from the original apostolic message seems to be quite justified. Rather than ascribing to Irenaeus and other defenders of orthodoxy such negative motives as fear of a loss of personal or ecclesiastical power[17] or dismissing their actions by using pejorative terms such as "heresy-hunters," we should try to understand them from the perspective of how they saw themselves. Due to the radical differences between the Gnostic and the orthodox views of the Christian faith, Irenaeus and other defenders of the faith believed it was necessary to condemn Gnostic teachings. Irenaeus and others did not attack works that supported the teaching of the first-century writings, but they were concerned when anyone or any work tried to redefine what the earliest founders of the faith had set out as the life and message of Jesus. In their minds, the apostles had established the faith in the first few decades, and that faith could not be redefined or reshaped by any subsequent writers.

At this point, we return again to the issue of bias. There is a significant difference between calling Irenaeus a "defender of the faith" or a "heresy hunter." Both terms, like any terms, can be problematic. The former term is usually used by those who side with Irenaeus and appreciate what he did for the church in its fight against heresy. The problem with such use is that it may reflect an uncritical acceptance of Irenaeus that borders on hagiography. The problem with the latter term is that it most likely reflects a bias that sides with the Gnostics and opposes the orthodox church in its claim to be the holder of the apostles' teaching. Whether this anti-orthodox bias is rooted in the Enlightenment's centuries-old at-

16. J. Gresham Machen, *Christianity and Liberalism* (New York: Macmillan, 1923; reprint, Grand Rapids: Eerdmans, 1987), 20.

17. For example, see Elaine Pagels, *The Gnostic Gospels* (London: Weidenfeld and Nicolson, 1979).

tack on the church's authority, an expression of a contemporary resurgence of Gnosticism in the West,[18] an ecumenical desire for peace among all religions (and thus, no one religion saying another is "wrong"), postmodern perspectivalism, or an unhappy experience in one's personal experience with the church, such a bias needs to be identified and critiqued. A great deal of contemporary critical scholarship shares this bias (despite the impression given that it is "objective" and "scholarly"), and the scholarship surrounding the *Gospel of Judas* and other Gnostic finds is usually based on this bias. Readers must note it and realize how such a bias influences one to take a very negative and critical approach to the orthodox church and a very positive attitude to the value of the *Gospel of Judas*.

18. In regard to Gnosticism in America, Harold Bloom writes:

> Religion will flourish among us, whether its devotees call it Mormonism, Protestantism, Catholicism, Islam, Judaism, or what-you-will. And the American Religion, for its two centuries of existence, seems to me irretrievably Gnostic. It is a knowing, by and of an uncreated self, or self-within-the-self, and the knowledge leads to freedom, a dangerous and doom-eager freedom: from nature, time, history, community, other selves. I shake my head in unhappy wonderment at the politically correct younger intellectuals, who hope to subvert what they cannot begin to understand, an obsessed society wholly in the grip of a dominant Gnosticism.

See Harold Bloom, *The American Religion: The Emergence of the Post-Christian Nation* (New York: Simon and Schuster, 1992), 49. See also Philip Lee, *Against the Protestant Gnostics* (Oxford: Oxford University Press, 1987).

Conclusion

By way of conclusion, we thought that we would conduct an interview with ourselves. We posed the following questions to each other in an attempt to gain better insight into what the discovery of the *Gospel of Judas* means individually, as collaborators on this project, and as those concerned for the life of the church and Christians who have been attracted to this document.

1. As a New Testament scholar, or as a church historian, what do you think that this find means?

Stanley: I believe that the *Gospel of Judas* means very little for New Testament study. As the discussion above indicates, there is little about the *Gospel of Judas* that has any direct bearing on the New Testament itself. The document itself dates to the third or probably fourth century. It may be a later copy of an earlier second-century document, but certainly not any earlier than that. It is a piece of rehabilitation literature, which the Gnostics were so good at creating so that they could take those who were on the fringes of Christianity and rehabilitate them to positions central to their belief system. As we have noted above, the *Gospel of Judas* itself knows that Judas is guilty of selling Jesus out for money, that he was Jesus' betrayer, and that he incurred the wrath of Jesus' closest followers, the disciples. The *Gospel of Judas* as much as says this, which is an explicit admission that it accepts the New Testament account, even if it attempts to transform it in another context. What I see from this is that the New Testament account was firmly established, widely believed and firmly held, and that even the Gnostics who were intent on trying to displace it had very little strength to their arguments.

There are a number of ways in which the *Gospel of Judas* has value and rewards study, however. One is that it offers a further piece of Gnostic literature. We have significant finds from Nag Hammadi, but now with these four documents from Al Minya — two of which are virtually the same as two already known from Nag Hammadi — we see that there was a corpus of materials associated with the Gnostics of the time. It helps us to understand what they believed and how they believed it. A further benefit of the *Gospel of Judas* is that it gives us some idea of some of the later interpretation of what Judas did. As we have noted above, there have been a variety of responses to Judas and his betrayal of Jesus. Some vilified him and others — going far too far in condemning wider groups for the terrible mistakes of one man — while others have tried to exonerate him — straying too far in the other direction. Nevertheless, all of these interpretations give us insight into how people later thought about Judas and reacted to him. The Gnostics, so we were told as early as Irenaeus and now know to be the case, were one of those groups. We see now what one of their responses was. It is a unique response in that this is the only *Gospel of Judas* that we have. However, it is a very predictable response in that the *Gospel of Judas* itself is a fairly typical piece of Gnostic literature of the time.

Gordon: We have been fortunate in the last century to have so many important and exciting discoveries of manuscripts — some that we have never seen before, and others that no one had mentioned for over fifteen hundred years. The recent discovery of the *Gospel of Judas* is just one more of these fascinating discoveries.

Probably the greatest threat the church faced in the second century was Gnosticism. Gnosticism had a variety of Christian-looking documents and dynamic and persuasive leaders who claimed that they had the real truth of Jesus Christ and were the ones with the real apostolic message. In the case of Marcion, they even had their own canon. The discovery of the *Gospel of Judas* provides us with an even greater awareness of the types of challenges that the church faced. The content and genre of the *Gospel of Judas* certainly shed some light on one type of second-century Gnosticism. It also provides some important insight into the type of rehabilitation of marginal figures that the Cainites were known for. The *Gospel of Judas* was a provocative challenge to the traditional understanding of the Passion events, and no doubt would have caused some consternation among early Christians who were a bit perplexed about hearing about the hero Judas.

2. What would you say to those who have said that the *Gospel of Judas* threatens to overturn traditional Christianity or at least its view of Judas?

Stanley: I think that such people ought to sit down and recompose themselves. It is no doubt true that the *Gospel of Judas* attempts to overturn the traditional and — I would strongly repeat — biblical account of Judas's betrayal, but that it fails by granting the case that he is the betrayer. If anything is turned on its head, it is the Gnostic attempt to rehabilitate Judas by its admission that he is guilty. This document, however, is just one of several that have recently been heralded as the greatest discovery since, well, the last great discovery that we had a few weeks earlier. So much hyperbole cannot be good for one's heart — it certainly is not good for one's scholarly credibility to be flying off half-cocked every few weeks claiming to have established a revisionist Christianity when the evidence is so flawed or lacking. There have no doubt been many significant archaeological and textual finds in the last hundred years or so — but the most important ones have not overturned traditional Christian views. To the contrary, they have shown that there is a firm textual basis for the Christian Scriptures, that the practices and beliefs reflected in the New Testament are consonant with the practices and beliefs of the times at least as reflected by other religious groups, and that there are good reasons why what we call orthodox Christianity is just that. It was not a battle of equally valid forms of Christianity, but the clear emergence of belief and texts that went back to the earliest days of Christianity and its founders.

Gordon: I understand some people's desire to free Judas from some of the damning indictments and caricatures that have existed in the past. I am sympathetic toward those who are repulsed and saddened by some of the church's sins of the past, and I can appreciate the hope that these documents will lead us to a freer and less authoritarian Christianity. I am also quite aware of the power of postmodern relativism that shudders at the thought that one religion would dare to make the claim that it is right and others are wrong.

Nevertheless, I am convinced that much of the hopes for Gnostic documents in general and the *Gospel of Judas* in particular cannot be supported from the evidence. First, there is no reason to think that the church would have been any better off with these texts being the basis for the faith. I like what Jenkins has to say on this matter:

> The medieval church has been criticized for many failings, prominent among which would be clerical elitism, anti-Semitism, misogyny, an excessive taste for theological quibbling, and a rejection of the natural world. Since these sins were already so rife, or at least emerging, in Gnostic texts before 250, it is unlikely that a hypothetical Gnostic church would have been any better. It would likely have been far worse. We would have to imagine a Gnostic Christianity that not only practiced these failings, but amply justified them from their scriptures. The movement would also have been utterly submerged in magic and occult speculation. Just what aspect of Gnosticism should we feel sorry to have lost?[1]

Second, there is no reason to think that the *Gospel of Judas* "transforms our understanding of the New Testament events," or "challenges

---

1. Philip Jenkins, *Hidden Gospels: How the Search for Jesus Lost Its Way* (New York: Oxford University Press, 2001), 212.

our deepest held views," or "creates a crisis of faith." No, for those who know their church history there is good reason to believe that the orthodox church, not the Gnostics, is the holder of the apostolic tradition. The orthodox church's texts, creeds, documents, and tradition all pre-date Gnosticism by generations. By all fair accounts one must conclude that Gnosticism was not just another equally valid form of the faith, but a radical departure from the apostolic faith that had been preserved and passed down in the orthodox church.

3. Why did you undertake to write this book, if you are so negative on the value of the *Gospel of Judas?*

Stanley: I am a New Testament scholar, and I could see early on that this document has little to offer a student of the New Testament. The opportunity to work with my colleague Gordon gave us the chance to undertake a much more thorough and wide-ranging analysis to take into account the early church and the emergence of Gnosticism itself. To be frank, I was taken aback by the kinds of claims that were being made about this document by people who should have known better once they knew the facts. We thought that the record needed to be set straight. There were no doubt going to be some sincere Christians who were not aware of the developments of early Christianity, who might have been misled by the hyperbolic claims made about the *Gospel of Judas,* and we thought that by clearing the air and laying out what we think is the case about this document within the development of early Christianity we could provide a service to the church of today. Christians of today do not need to fear that the New Testament got it wrong on Judas or Jesus or whatever, but can continue to believe that the Scriptures in fact do preserve an accurate account of what Judas did — as the *Gospel of Judas* clearly reveals if you understand what the document admits to.

Gordon: I do not think that I am negative toward it. I just do not buy into the assumptions that compel one to reinterpret the traditional understanding of the orthodox church's struggle with Gnosticism. As I mentioned above, there is some scholarly value to the *Gospel of Judas*.

On a more positive note, one personal reason for writing this book is to provide an alternative interpretation of the significance of the *Gospel of Judas*. Along with many others I was looking forward to the release of the text of the gospel. I was disappointed (but not surprised), however, by the sensationalized commentary surrounding the release of the document. Due to my disappointment, we sought to provide a thoughtful commentary on the discovery that was not driven by a contemporary agenda and/or radical modern criticism. Of course, our bias is obviously for the orthodox. However, I also believe that there are legitimate reasons to argue for a more traditional understanding of Gnostic writings such as the *Gospel of Judas*.

Selected Reading

Roger S. Bagnall, *Reading Papyri, Writing Ancient History* (New York: Routledge, 1995).

David Bebbington, *Patterns in History: A Christian Perspective on Historical Thought* (Leicester: Apollos, 1990).

Craig Blomberg, *The Historical Reliability of the Gospels* (Downers Grove: InterVarsity, 1987).

Colin Brown, *Miracles and the Critical Mind* (Grand Rapids: Eerdmans, 1984).

F. F. Bruce, *The Canon of Scripture* (Downers Grove: InterVarsity, 1988).

F. F. Bruce, *The New Testament Documents: Are They Reliable?* (Downers Grove: InterVarsity, 1972).

Craig A. Evans, *Jesus and the Ossuaries* (Waco: Baylor University Press, 2003).

Craig A. Evans and Stanley E. Porter, eds., *Dictionary of New Testament Background* (Downers Grove: InterVarsity, 2000).

David Ewert, *From Ancient Tablets to Modern Translations: A General Introduction to the Bible* (Grand Rapids: Zondervan, 1983).

W. H. C. Frend, *The Early Church* (Minneapolis: Fortress, 1991).

Robert M. Grant, *Gnosticism and Early Christianity* (second ed.; New York: Columbia University Press, 1966).

Arland J. Hultgren and Steven A. Haggmark, eds., *The Earliest Christian Heretics: Readings from Their Opponents* (Minneapolis: Fortress, 1996).

Philip Jenkins, *Hidden Gospels: How the Search for Jesus Lost Its Way* (New York: Oxford University Press, 2001).

Hans Jonas, *The Gnostic Religion: The Message of the Alien God and the Beginnings of Christianity* (second ed.; Boston: Beacon, 1963).

Rodolphe Kasser, Marvin Meyer, and Gregor Wurst, eds., *The Gospel of Judas from Codex Tchacos* (Washington: National Geographic, 2006).

William Klassen, *Judas: Betrayer or Friend of Jesus?* (Minneapolis: Fortress, 1996).

Herbert Krosney, *The Lost Gospel: The Quest for the Gospel of Judas Iscariot* (Washington: National Geographic, 2006).

Bentley Layton, *The Gnostic Scriptures* (Garden City: Doubleday, 1987).

Bruce M. Metzger, *The Early Versions of the New Testament* (London: Oxford University Press, 1975).

Kim Paffenroth, *Judas: Images of the Lost Disciple* (Louisville: Westminster/John Knox, 2001).

Stanley E. Porter, "Paul and the Process of Canonization," in Craig A. Evans and Emanuel Tov, eds., *Exploring the Origins of the Bible* (Grand Rapids: Baker, in press).

James M. Robinson, *The Secrets of Judas: The Story of the Misunderstood Disciple and His Lost Gospel* (San Francisco: HarperCollins, 2006).

James M. Robinson, ed., *The Nag Hammadi Library in English* (San Francisco: Harper and Row, 1988).

Riemer Roukema, *Gnosis and Faith in Early Christianity: An Introduction to Gnosticism* (Harrisburg: Trinity, 1999).

Kurt Rudolph, *Gnosis: The Nature and History of Gnosticism* (trans. Robin McL. Wilson; San Francisco: Harper, 1987).

Eric G. Turner, *Greek Papyri: An Introduction* (Oxford: Clarendon, 1968).

Gerard Vallee, *A Study in Anti-Gnostic Polemics: Irenaeus, Hippolytus, and Epiphanius* (Waterloo: Wilfrid Laurier University Press, 1981).

Michael J. Wilkins and J. P. Moreland, eds., *Jesus under Fire: Modern Scholarship Reinvents the Historical Jesus* (Grand Rapids: Zondervan, 1995).

N. T. Wright, *The Resurrection of the Son of God* (Minneapolis: Fortress, 2004).

Index of Modern Authors

Index of Ancient Sources